A SURVIVAL GUIDE FOR STAGE MANAGERS

A Practical Step-by-Step Handbook To Stage Management

Mary Ellen Allison

Outskirts Press, Inc.
Denver, Colorado

COPY EDITOR: Mayra David
COVER PHOTOS by Hanna Allison

The opinions expressed in this manuscript are solely the opinions of the author and do not represent the opinions or thoughts of the publisher. The author has represented and warranted full ownership and/or legal right to publish all the materials in this book.

A Survival Guide for Stage Managers
A Practical Step-by-Step Handbook to Stage Management
All Rights Reserved.
Copyright © 2011 Mary Ellen Allison

Grateful acknowledgement for permission to reprint excerpts from *Some Sweet Day:*
Book by Don Jones and Mac Pirkle
    Copyright by Don Jones and Mac Pirkle. All rights reserved.
Music and Lyrics by Si Kahn
    Copyright by Joe Hill Music LLC. All rights reserved.
For information about producing *Some Sweet Day,*
    please contact Si Kahn (sikahn@bellsouth.net)

Outskirts Press, Inc.
http://www.outskirtspress.com

ISBN: 978-1-4327-6651-1
Library of Congress Control Number: 2010940562

Outskirts Press and the "OP" logo are trademarks belonging to Outskirts Press, Inc.

PRINTED IN THE UNITED STATES OF AMERICA

DEDICATION

For my daughter, Hanna: my best and favorite production, my light and hope.

For my sister, Sara: who taught me to dream and to live every moment that we are given to the fullest.

For my family: who always supported me in my endeavors and instilled in me the ability to organize a large group of diverse persons with differing agendas.

CONTENTS

PART TWO: REHEARSAL PROCESS

PART THREE: TECHNICAL ASPECTS

PART FOUR: PERFORMANCES

PART FIVE: THE CAREER

PREFACE

Often in the educational and community theatre world, the young "get up and go" person is given the job of stage managing, even though they have no experience in this very demanding, leadership position. As such, I thought it would be helpful for those of you with little or no experience to have a simple and direct guidebook to aid you through the hard times of your first stage managing position.

When I was a junior in college (having finally decided to make it official and major in theatre), I was asked by a graduate student director what position I would like on his mainstage show. I responded, "lighting designer". He said, "taken". I said, "assistant director." He said, "Taken". I said, "How about stage manager?" He said, "You're hired." Thus began a career in stage management. To this day, I believe he knew me better than I knew myself. The show was *The Wizard of Oz*, a musical with twenty munchkins, multiple sets, over two hundred light cues, pyrotechnics and a dog that needed walking at intermission and at breaks. (A job I willingly volunteered for in order to get five minutes of "quiet time".) I have now stage managed for over thirty years and over one hundred shows. These include numerous musicals, original plays, and venues from outdoor dramas to Broadway. I have seen my students, interns and assistants develop their abilities and then work in the professional world, also from outdoor dramas to Broadway. It is very exciting to me to have had a hand (albeit slight) in their development. I only hope that you will have the same success in your chosen field. Shortly, those of you who are stage managing for the first time should know if it is the job for you. I wish you luck.

My objective with this book is to give you—the novice stage manager—a concise handbook that details the multiple functions and responsibilities of the stage manager. Included are chapters on all the numerous jobs which the stage manager must understand (from directing to designing) as well as the myriad of functions that they must accomplish to survive in the theatre. I believe that by using this handbook as a guide, the novice will have the most often asked questions answered and the stage manager with little experience will receive positive reinforcement that they are going in the right direction.

ACKNOWLEDGEMENTS

I would like to thank the directors, assistant stage managers, students, and interns, who have worked with me over the years and shared their knowledge and excitement of the theatre. I won't list them all as there are so many: you know who you are.

Special thanks to: Kevin Lanham for realizing that I would love stage managing; Nick Rinaldi for hiring a *novice* stage manager because of my *potential*; and Celeste Hall, who trusted my judgement and helped me realize that I was a good stage manager.

I was lucky to have two special teachers at Western Kentucky University: Bill Leonard and Jim Brown; who taught me to be a well-rounded theatre artist.

Thanks to Si Kahn, Mac Pirkle and Don Jones for allowing me to use portions of their wonderful musical, *Some Sweet Day*, in my examples.

Thanks to my friends for being so supportive through the process, especially: Laura Lindson, Jennifer and Jillian Poste, Pat Moore, Denise Regan, Maria Vail, Kristina Madsen, Andrea Yoson, and Lisa Foreman.

A very special thanks to Mayra David, who came to my rescue and brought her expertise to this project. She pushed me to surpass my own expectations. I can never thank her enough.

Most importantly, I want to thank my beautiful daughter, Hanna. She dealt with my fears and tears, and made me dinner when I was chained to the computer. All my love.

INTRODUCTION

You cannot teach stage management out of a book. You cannot learn it all during one course or while sitting around talking about it. You have to get out there and do it. There is nothing better than experience.

One of the things you will learn to love about stage managing is that it is always changing. It is a new learning experience every show you do. You always get different problems, different personalities, and different situations.

So: are you going to learn everything there is to know about stage managing by the end of this book? No. You'll get an idea of how hard the job can be and you'll get a basis from which to start. You can apply the information learned here and hopefully develop your own approach to stage managing.

I will be using examples from the musical *Some Sweet Day*, music and lyrics by Si Kahn, book by Mac Pircle and Don Jones, throughout the book.

THEATRE HIERARCHY

In order to understand the job of the stage manager, you must understand the hierarchy of theatre practitioners. Everyone has their own position to fill. You need to figure out where every person fits in the hierarchy of the theatre where you are employed. If you know each person's job, you will know who is responsible for every aspect of the theatrical process. It is successful communication between all members of the production that leads to an enjoyable working environment.

The stage manager is a facilitator. It is their main function to make sure the work of others is accomplished. In order to do that, it is important to understand where the stage manager fits in a hierarchical view of the theatre world. I will go into greater detail on these working relationships later, but an overview is essential at this point.

We will look at the hierchy as a pyramid-like structure.

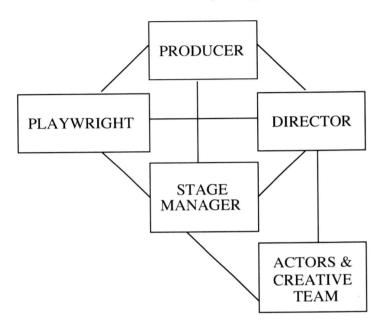

SM TIP: This diagram only includes part of the theatrical structure and is a generalization regarding theatre. Every theatre is a little different because of the experiences of the people who work there. You must openly communicate with all the collaborators.

As a facilitator, open and positive communication is a crucial part of making the show a success and the process a lot nicer for all involved. Any disruption of the lines between the stage manager and any of the other members of the hierarchy will ultimately lead to problems for the production.

THE PRODUCER

The top of the pyramid is always the producer. As the 0person responsible for choosing plays, hiring creative staff, and finding funding, it is rather obvious that these functions put them in the forefront of authority. The stage manager must serve the producer as the person responsible for making sure that the production goes along as scheduled. Never forget you work for the producer.

In an educational situation, the director is usually the producer. The director makes a lot of the decisions that the producer would in the professional world. The same is often the case in a community theatre. The producer will: often choose the show; hire the director, designers and choreographer; and may choose the cast.

THE DIRECTOR

The next level in the hierarchy is the director. They are the creative backbone of a production, and it is your job to make sure that their vision gets on the stage. Therefore, from a creative side, your job is often to act as liaison between the director and all others.

THE CREATIVE STAFF

The creative staff (set, costume and lighting designers, as well as choreographers and music directors) are the next step on the pyramid. It is imperative that you understand how each of the positions, from designers to choreographers, fit into the scheme of the production and how each of them perform their own functions. You do not need to be able to perform all their jobs, but you must be able to communicate with them.

THE PLAYWRIGHT

Most often, you will not be working with the playwright. If you happen to be working on a new play, and the playwright is present, they will be on the same level as the director, but the playwright will more than likely go to, and through, the director for any comments or suggestions that will affect your job. The playwright should not be giving you or the actors notes, unless you have arranged that with the director.

THE STAGE MANAGER
The next level in the hierarchy is the stage manager, who will be directly responsible for the actors and the crew. Working with actors and crew is one of the most important jobs that a stage manager accomplishes. It is your responsibility to keep the lines of communication open between yourself and all the other members of the team.

THE ACTORS
The actors will be doing what the director asks of them. As the stage manager, you will organize them so they know: when they have to be somewhere, where they have to be , what they will be doing when they get there, and when they get breaks. Because you work so closely with the actors, it is imperative that they understand that you are going to help them throughout the process.

PERSONALITY TRAITS
If you are looking to decide if this is a job that you would be suited for, why not look at some personality traits of a person who should NOT attempt the job of stage manager?

1.   The person who wants total control.   The stage manager has the appearance of being in control, but they really aren't.   The producer and the director are the ultimate decision makers.   Even the actor is out of your control.   It looks like you are in control but that is an illusion.   If you want control, and you want to be a dictator, it's not really the right kind of position for you, because theatre is a collaborative art.   Even the paper work and organization for which you are responsible is a collaborative part of the theatrical process.

2.   The person who needs to receive affirmation of their good work.   Although you may get a "job well done", most directors and producers and other theatre artists take it for granted that you will do a good job.   It is when you mess up that you will hear it (and rightfully so).   Very seldom does someone tell you what a good job you are doing.   It is a thankless job.

There are times when you know you are doing a good job, yet all you are getting is flak from people because they forget that you are a novice stage manager. After getting through the first weeks of rehearsal without any problems, they now think you know everything there is to know about stage managing. Doing the job over and over will help the learning process, but every day there is going to be something new to learn.

3. The person who can't take criticism and always has an excuse. If something goes wrong, whether or not it is your fault, the one thing you don't want to do is give excuses. Directors don't want to hear excuses, they want to hear "I will deal with it". An "I'll fix it." instead of an excuse works wonders. As long as you follow through and fix it. Directors, designers, and producers want to see you working hard and not making the same mistakes over and over. If they see that you are trying to do your best, most people will say "okay, fine", but they still aren't going to pat you on the back and tell you that you did a good job. If you always start with "but I meant to..." or "I don't think...", don't even try stage managing. It is not a place for excuse makers. Take the notes you are given and do the task right the next time.

4. The person who has to take time to think through a situation several times before making a decision. Or someone who waits for someone else to make the decisions. You must be able to think on your feet. The situation is always changing. You have to be able to make split second decisions and not say, "Okay.... Well.... I'll go see who thinks this and who thinks that". You need to actually make decisions. This is a double-edged sword when you are working in an educational or community theatre situation. If you take the initiative and make the decisions, sometimes you can get called out because you are a student and "you aren't supposed to make decisions".

At some point you may end up working with a director (not very often in the professional theatre) who doesn't want you to make decisions. They want to make all the decisions themselves. If a show has opened and is running, nobody can make decisions for you. If there is a problem backstage, you have to deal with it. If the director is sitting in the audience, in the middle of the fifth row, they cannot get up, come backstage and fix a problem. You have to be the one who is figuring out the best solution.

> SM EXPERIENCE: Because of my background as a stage manager, when I direct, I tend to like stage managers that make decisions, even if they make bad ones. To me a bad decision is still better than no decision.

5. The person who is laid back and lets the world come to them. The stage manager must be a go getter. You cannot wait for someone to tell you what to do. You must anticipate it and then do it. If you sit back passively and let everybody else do the job, you are going to have problems stage managing. Stage managing is an active position. You have to get out there and "just do it". You cannot sit and wait for the director to say, "Excuse me, we are doing this scene and you have to set up." You have to be thinking ahead. Although you spend a lot of time sitting behind desks, stage managing is not a "sit behind the desk" position. You have to think ahead about what has to happen. You cannot wait: you have to anticipate. And then do it.

6. The person who must have a say in all discussions. The stage manager is a facilitator. It is your job to help others develop their visions. Every once in a while, you can make a suggestion. But when the designers and the director are discussing the designs, you should keep your mouth shut. When the actors and the director are in a discussion about character, you should keep your mouth shut. It is not your job and not your position to make comments on what everyone else does. Keep your mouth shut and let the director do their job. It does not mean you cannot ask questions, but you have to watch what you say. If a director asks for your opinion, give it. But, a director will get really tired of a stage manager that is constantly saying, "What if you do it this way?" or "What if you do that?"

ATTRIBUTES FOR SUCCESS

If any of the previous comments apply to you, maybe you should rethink taking this job. But if you are still interested, take a look at some of the attributes you need, to be a successful stage manager. A partial list includes:

1. Patience.
2. More patience.
3. Even more patience.
4. Ability to stay calm in a trying situation. Throughout the theatrical process, you will encounter moments of stress. You must be able to deal with them calmly and with authority. The stress level in stage managing is unbelievably high and you have to figure out how to deal with it, whether it be by doing yoga everyday or leaving the rehearsal space for a few minutes during breaks. As a stage manager you very seldom get a break. You can call a ten minute break and then six people want to come and talk to you or the director says *we need to deal with this or that.* Sometimes, when the stress level is high you have to say, "I need to take a break". In which case, you take a five minute break out of the ten minutes because you need the other five to deal with the situation of the moment. You cannot be a stressful person in a rehearsal situation.

5. Endurance. Both physically and mentally. Make sure you get to bed at night and sleep. In the educational world most students are young and have a lot of endurance. You come home, you do your homework, you sit in front of the computer till 3:00 in the morning, you get four hours sleep and start all over again. That is fine, but it does not do very well for your endurance when it comes around to technical rehearsals and you are exhausted from the start. That is when you have to mentally be at the top of your game. You'll find that in a professional situation, people do not go out often and they do not have a tendency to "party". The actors are doing their homework, learning their lines. You are doing your homework, organizing the paperwork. Everybody is trying to get as much sleep as they possibly can. Sometimes, that is not a lot—but, you get as much as possible.

6. A sense of humor. About the work and yourself.

You need a sense of humor in order to survive. Laughter will help release the stress of the position. Do not laugh at inappropriate times, but do not feel you must always have a serious attitude. Take the work seriously, but enjoy it at the same time.

7. Good Organizational skills. Great organizational skills should probably be listed as number one. It does not mean you keep your apartment immaculate. An obsessive compulsive personality is not a requirement. It helps. But it is not required. It is your organizational skills that will keep the show going on a smooth course. You are not just organizing yourself, but everyone associated with the show. The director needs to feel that the show is in good hands, once it opens. That feeling must begin the first moment you start working on the show.

8. You need the ability to empathize with whoever you are working with at the time—auditionees, directors, actors. A good stage manager has the ability to understand what another person is going through. This does not mean to agree with everyone, but let them know that you understand their situation.

SM TIP: I recommend that student stage managers take every kind of theatre class (acting, dance, tech, design, directing), as well as, psychology, and sociology classes. The more you understand about the other person's job and the more you understand about people, the easier it is for you to deal with the problems you will face, effectively.

9. Leadership skills. If you have not had stage management experience, have you had any leadership experience? Running a club, or something? Always remember that the good leader gets the best out of those with whom they work. Never forget that the ultimate leader is the director. You are the right hand of the director. Your job is to use your skills to make their vision a success.

10. An ability to mediate, to be someone's surrogate therapist, brother, sister, mother, referee, father, etc. Take psychology classes, sociology classes, social work classes: try to understand how to deal with people, because that is what you are

doing more than anything else.

11. Must "play well with others". Even if you dislike someone, they should never know it. You should go out of your way to be nice to people that you do not personally like because it is your job to get along with all those with whom you work.

12. An inherent love of theatre. I do not know how anyone could do this job if they did not love every aspect of the theatrical process. I do not know anybody in any aspect of theatre who does not love it for one reason or another.

So now you are thinking, "I'm this person. I can stage manage." Let us look at the the function and responsibilities of the stage manager.

FUNCTION AND RESPONSIBITIES

A stage manager has numerous responsibilities, but only one function: to make a show run smoothly throughout the process from preproduction to closing night. It is that simple, yet that complicated. It is the job that most people outside the theatre world have no idea what it is. It is a job that, if done well, makes everyone else look good. The purpose of this book is to give a concise analysis of all the responsibilities inherent in the position.

Above all, the stage manager must be given the authority to perform the responsibilities laid on them. Herein lies the black hole of stage managing in an educational or community theatre situation. As a novice, you often must prove to your superiors (director and producer) that you are capable of being a leader. Many times the person who is your superior has never actually had a competent stage manager and has no idea how to go about letting a stage manager do their job. Unfortunately, many a good stage manager does not get that "ultimate" experience until they work professionally. In the professional world, you are expected to do your job. You are given the responsibility and the authority to make it happen.

PART ONE

ORGANIZATION

CHAPTER ONE

☑ PREPRODUCTION WORK

You have been asked to perform the function of stage managing your college, community, or high school production. Where do you start? With the script. You must immediately obtain a copy from the producer, director or teacher. Read it. Do not try to analyze it. Just read it. Do not let the number of set changes, props, or actors scare you. You will handle all of them as they come. This first reading is the only opportunity you will have to get a true "first impression" of the play. Enjoy the read and see if you "enjoy" the play.

Before rehearsals begin, you must get organized. The more work you can do pre-rehearsal, the better prepared you will be when they begin. You have to get familiar with every part of the script, the production, and the theatre itself.

TECHNICAL LISTS

After reading through the script once, read through it again. This time make lists of all the technical aspects that are named, commented on or described in the script. Read through the script slowly and make notes – on separate pieces of paper – of everything that you find concerning technical requirements. It is very helpful to have a separate list of each technical aspect (lights, sets, costumes, sound, etc.), so you can quickly check your notes for information.

What follows are examples of lists– using *Some Sweet Day*.

PROPS:

Make a table for the list of all the props, what scene and page they are used on, and the character using them. Leave room in the table to add comments and a note on whether you have found a rehearsal prop or the actual prop.

PRELIMINARY PROP LIST Date						
ACT ONE *SOME SWEET DAY* Page ___ of ___						

Scene	Page	Prop	Character	Note	Reh. Prop	Show Prop
1	1	Hoes	Field Workers	Used again	✔	✔
	1	Bucket		Used again	✔	✔
	2	Gun	Buddy	Carry it?	✔	
2	6	Jug	Buddy	Carry it?	✔	

SOUND CUES:

Make a table of every sound or noise that is listed or commented on by a character. You should note the page it happens on and who is probably responsible for making the sound (might be an actor – knocking).

PRELIMINARY SOUND LIST Date			
ACT ONE *SOME SWEET DAY* Page ___ of ___			

Scene	Page	Sound	Comments
1	1	Hoes hitting floor	Actors
1	2	Whistle	Buddy
4	21	Noise	Actor's name

LIGHTS:

In the lighting table, you need to note specific lighting needs, such as when a character says, "I see the sun coming up." You may never use this list, but it will make you aware of the lighting requirements.

PRELIMINARY LIGHTING LIST Date ACT ONE *SOME SWEET DAY* Page ___ of ___			
Scene	Page	Setting	Lighting Notes
1	1	Field	End of Work Day
2	8	Riverbank	Evening
3	13	Church Interior	Evening

SET PIECES:

Make a table for your list of set pieces that are noted in the script (such as chairs and table). You have not seen the set design yet, so you are going by what the playwright says in the script.

PRELIMINARY SETTINGS/SET PIECES Date ACT ONE *SOME SWEET DAY* Page ___ of ___				
Scene	Page	Setting	Set Pieces	Comments
1	1	Cotton Field	Cotton Field?	
2	8	Riverbank	Riverbank?	
3	13	Church	Benches	

COSTUMES:

You have yet to see the costume designs, so your table will be a listing of what it says in the script, e.g. a change for a

character into "church clothes". Note questions regarding whether something is a costume or a prop (e.g. a coat or a cane).

PRELIMINARY COSTUME CHANGES	Date
ACT ONE *SOME SWEET DAY*	Page ___ of ___

Scene	Page	Character	Costume
3	13	Field Hands	From Work - Church
4	21	Jessup	Into Grand Iawgan
		3 Actors	White Knights
5	24	Fob & Willetha	From Church - Work

ADDITIONAL LISTS:
        Your show may have other requirements. It could be
pyrotechnics or combat. You need to make a table similar to
those above that includes all questions you may have about any
other requirements mentioned in the script.

> SM TIP: These preliminary tech lists will include infor-
> mation that you need to know throughout the production
> process. Note anything that stands out as something that
> will be dealt with during the rehearsal, or anything you
> have a question about. Be flexible. All of these lists will
> change. You will be adding to and deleting from these lists
> throughout the rehearsal process.

MEET WITH DIRECTOR
        Schedule a meeting with the director. Be honest and tell
them that this is your first experience as stage manager. But also
tell them that you are very capable, a good learner and will work
very hard to do a good job. If you have not worked with the director previously, now would be a good time to ask what assistance they specifically need. Some directors organize their own

set changes. Others do not want to deal with it. Some want to keep in contact with staff and designers themselves, others prefer that you serve as liaison. Every director's style of working is different. Do not assume they will all be the same. What you must instill in them this first meeting, is a sense that you are there to make their lives easier and less complicated during the creative process. At this time, you can also give them a copy of your prop list and ask them if they would like to check it and/or add to it.

At this time you can also discuss the director's scheduling needs. Will they be using all the actors at every rehearsal? Will there be staggered calls (only four actors the first hour, the whole company the rest of the night)? Do they want you to figure out times of calls after they give you a list of what scenes will be rehearsed? How much time would they like to spend on each scene?

Find out what they would like to accomplish for the first rehearsal. A sample schedule for the first rehearsal with a five hour work day could be as follows:

6-6:15   Meet & greet—coffee & snack (measurements?)
6:15   Gather around the table and introductions
6:30   Director talks to all (ideas on the play)
7:00   Presentations by designers
7:30   First read through
10:00   Company meeting:
                 stage management business, collect bios
                 distribute rehearsal schedules, etc.
11:00   Break for the evening.

SM TIP: Careful about measurements. They take longer than scheduled. If it goes long, most directors will start to get "antsy". You may find yourself in a tight spot telling the director that they can't start the meeting until measurements are completed. If at all possible, the measurements should be done at another time.

REHEARSAL SCENES

The play may be a long one-act divided into many scenes or a full-length play with several acts. If it does not have scene divisions, the director may choose to divide it into rehearsal scenes. This could be done with "French scenes" (new scene when a character exits or enters) or the director may choose to divide it based on their own ideas on the play. The rehearsal schedule will be determined based on the scenes the director chooses. Go through your script and put a tab where every rehearsal scene begins. (Post-it notes work beautifully for this.)

> SM TIP: If it is possible to mark the rehearsal scenes in the scripts distributed to the actors, great! If not, you need to 1) type a list of the scene breaks, or 2) take 10 minutes at the first rehearsal to give the breaks to the cast. It is necessary that everyone is on the same page, literally.

SCENE BREAKDOWN

Organize a table of all the characters. This can be divided into men and women or from the biggest part to the smallest. Start with the *Scene Breakdown* heading and the show's title. Then, down the left side of the table, list: scene, page number (the page number where the scene begins), number of pages (total within the scene), and each character's name. Across the top, list the scene numbers for the first act.

At this time, go through the script page by page and, for each scene, note who is in it. Differentiate between characters in the scene who have lines and those who don't by placing an X under the scene in which the character has lines and an O under each scene in which they appear but have no lines. (The director may choose to rehearse with only speaking roles at some point).

SCENE BREAKDOWN *SOME SWEET DAY* ACT ONE							date		
Scene	1	2	3	4	5	6	7	8	9	10
Page #	1	8	13	21	25	28	33	39	46	49
# of pages	7	5	8	4	3	5	4	7	3	5
Sarah Jane	X		X			X		X		X
Isaac	X	X					X	X		
Fob	X		X		X	X		X	X	X
Emma	X		X			X	X	X		X
Willetha	X		X		X	X		X		X
Buddy	X	X						X	X	X
Jessup				X					X	X
Clea	X		X			X		X		X
Zachariah	X		X			X		X		X
Max	X		X			X		X		X
Reverend	X		X			X		X		X
Field hands	X					X		X		X
White Knights				X					X	X

You need to do the scene breakdown very carefully. Double-check your work as the rehearsal schedule, and those actors that are called for each rehearsal, will come from this sheet. You will see a pattern emerging as you fill in the slots under each scene for each character. Continue through all acts and scenes. You will use this sheet for organizing your rehearsal schedule.

> SM TIP: The scene breakdown is probably the most important form. You will use it throughout the rehearsal process. Make sure to double check that it is correct. Be aware that some directors will add actors into scenes during the rehearsal process. Make sure you update the scene breakdown if that occurs.

ORGANIZING THE SCRIPTS

Organizing the scripts is one of the first responsibilities of the stage manager. You must make sure that there are copies for the cast and crew as well as stage management copies for rehearsals (the prompt script) and "calling the show" (the cue script). How copies are made is determined by the type of script.

ORIGINAL SCRIPTS

In some theatres, there are office staff who have the responsibility of organizing and copying the scripts for the actors and staff. That means, you must make sure this is happening in a timely manner and that enough copies are being made. Sometimes, you have to take over this job. Having the right number of scripts available at the right time is of the utmost importance.

You must make sure the scripts are organized correctly, the holes are punched and the scripts are bound for the actors, designers, crew, etc. This is an expense that should come out of the stage management budget.

ORDERING SCRIPTS FROM A PUBLISHING HOUSE

If you are doing a published script (not an original), the producer will have secured the rights and may have already ordered the scripts. If they have not been ordered, find out who will be doing it. You may be the one responsible. If it is you, order them ASAP. You need to order enough copies for the entire creative staff, the cast, yourself, the director, and a couple extras for emergency situations (e.g. replacing an actor).

SM TIP: Once the scripts are copied, you can personalize them for the cast and crew. You can neatly put everyone's name on their binder and if you are so inclined, you can insert a flyer for the show as the first page, or inside the sleeve of the front of the binder. Because you are organizing the scripts, you can also insert any cast or crew handouts into their copies.

PROMPT BOOK

The prompt book is the most important element of keeping a stage manager organized. Everything you use on the production will be in the prompt book. Once you have a copy of the script, you must put it into prompt book form. If it is an original script, it should be ready for your binder. If it is in book form from a publisher, you must work to put the script into the proper form for stage management. There are several ways to do this: two "old style" and two "new style".

Old Style—

1) You can cut the outside binder off the script and glue the pages to letter-size paper that have a "window" cut out of the middle one inch smaller than the size of the script page. Then, you take a glue stick and glue down one side of the script page: when you turn the page over, you can see the other side of the page through the window.

2) You can cut up two copies of the script and glue each page side to letter-size paper. The problem with doing this is that the prompt script then is three times thicker than a normal script and it is similar to writing on a mound of paper.

New Style—

1) If it is a new show and there is enough time, you can type the script into a computer as a word document. It will familiarize you with every word of the play. You need to make sure the pages have the same text and page numbers as the copy the actors will be using.

2) As long as a copy has been purchased for each person that needs one, it is okay to enlarge or copy the script in such a way that will suit your needs. That means that you can copy one

page of a 5.25" X 7.25" script onto a 8.5" X 11" sheet of paper. The copied script is supposed to be destroyed after the show is completed.

COPYING A SCRIPT

Copying a script is a tedious process if you want to make sure the copies are clear and free of "black lines" created by the frame of original page size. You can use two blank pieces of paper and create an L-shaped "template" on the copy machine surface so that all you have to do is hold the open script in place next to it. Line up the spine of the actual script along the edge of the copy plate with the L-shaped template running down one side and the bottom edge of the script. By doing this the "black line" around the script is eliminated and it will give you over 3 inches of blank paper space to the right of the script text. This will be enough room for you to take blocking notation. Remember to move the template to the left side when you are copying the left side of the script. Otherwise, you end up with 3 inches of blank paper to the *left* of the script text on one page, and to the *right* of the script text on the next. This is fine if you are left handed, but most people will want the blank space on the right side. The way to make this tedious process a little less time consuming is to take a mat knife and cut off the binding of the script, so that the pages are loose.

You can also make a C-shaped template that has a small piece of paper at the top and the bottom, as well as down one side. Your copied script will sit in the middle of a letter-size sheet of paper. Tape the template to the copy machine surface with scotch tape. Make sure to move the book from one side to the next, so that the extra 3 inches of blank space are on the same side of each page once you have completed copying the script. This template gives you extra space on both the top and bottom of each page for blocking, cues or any other notes that will be needed. Don't forget to remove the scotch tape when you are finished.

Whichever method you use to copy the script, do a test of the first few pages to make sure the appearance is the way you want it.

COMPANY HANDBOOKS

You may work for an established theatre company and they may have a prepared package of information specifically for the cast and crew of each show. If this is available, you should secure a copy and go through it to make sure you understand all aspects. Then, if an actor asks a question, you can answer it. Sometimes you will get an actor with a question that will stump you. Be honest and tell them you don't know the answer, but that you will find out. Then, do so.

If the company does not have an organized handbook, it may be to your advantage to put one together. This is often done by the company manager, but not all theatres have that position. Anything you do in this area to help your cast and crew will be greatly appreciated.

The company handbook could contain any of the following information:

-Payroll (when you get paid)
-Banks (where you can cash your checks)
-Company policy regarding housing
-Company policy regarding complimentary tickets

Additional information about the area near the theatre:

-Where to get clothes laundered
-Restaurants and other places of business

SM EXPERIENCE: I did *Two Gentlemen of Verona*—the Globe Theatre Co. joint production with Theatre For A New Audience in NYC. (Although there was a British SM, Equity required an American one too.) One of my jobs in this unique situation was to get everything ready for the cast arrival. I added things to the co. handbook like: restaurant menus, subway maps, and where to find the London papers. I even stocked their apartments with breakfast foods (they were due to arrive at 1:00am). I did for them what I would hope someone would do for me. All of it endeared me to the cast.

PRODUCTION CONTACT SHEET

The production contact sheet should include the name, the position on the show, phone numbers, and email addresses of all members of the production staff. This should include the producer, director, stage managers, designers, and crew that are known. Find out if the producer wants their number on this list. It is important to start this list early in the process and distribute it immediately. The lines of communication are open from the beginning. Make the contact sheet clear and easy to read. When you update the contact sheet, make sure to date it so everyone knows which sheet is the most recent.

PRODUCTION CONTACT SHEET date *SOME SWEET DAY*		
Harry Alston (Director)	Email address	(C) 123-456-7890 (H)123-456-7891
John Smith (Stage Mgr.)	Email address	(C) 234-567-8910
Jerry Lanham (Music Director)	Email address	(C) 345-678-9101
Si Togo (Choreographer)	Email address	(Cell) 456-789-1011

PRODUCTION MEETINGS

Production meetings are held throughout to help organize and prevent communication misunderstandings for the creative process. All members of the design staff, as well as the director, technical directors and the stage managers should be present. As the stage manager, you may be in charge of these meetings. Sometimes you will have a production manager and they will be in charge.

During the first meeting you should make sure to cover all the dates on the schedule and the needs of the staff. The following is a list of work that possibly needs to be accomplished at this meeting:

-Collect paperwork from your designers (e.g. bios)
-Distribute contact sheet (check that info is correct)
-Distribute production calender (months until open)
You will either inform the designers of the dates or you will fill in the dates for the following:
-Date for "run through" for the designers
-Preliminary and final design deadlines
-Light hang and focus dates
-Set building/set construction deadlines
-Costume deadlines
-Dry tech
-Dress rehearsals
-Costume parade
-First Rehearsal with Orchestra
-Opening/Final dress rehearsal
Make sure each designer knows when they are needed at rehearsals. Do not assume they will know to be there.

Usually this meeting is all about deadlines. You can come into it with dates already determined by the producer or production manager. In which case, you are letting the staff know their deadlines. If no actual deadlines have been set, then the staff will have some input. It will all center around the opening date. Most theatres have a standard set of deadlines they use for every show.

PRODUCTION SCHEDULE

It is important that, from the beginning, everyone involved on the design side of the production understand the deadlines for their work. Most theatres will have a schedule in place that they impose on every production. Every deadline, for everything from rough drafts to final drawings, from electrical plots to "hang and focus", should be on this schedule. In addition, it will have dates for technical rehearsals, dress rehearsals, previews and opening night. This will give all members of the design team an overview of the entire design process. If the theatre does not have a set schedule, you need to make sure that the dates are thought out and instituted on your production.

The production schedule can be done on a calendar (production calendar) with the events typed into the appropriate date, or they can be written as a listing of important dates. For musicals, you would also have listed the first rehearsal with the orchestra and whether they are called for tech rehearsals.

PRODUCTION SCHEDULE date		
SHOW TITLE		
TECH REQUIREMENT	DATES	NOTES
Preliminary Set Designs	9/10/10	
Final Set Design	9/24/10	
Final Set Drawings	10/8/10	
Lighting Design	10/16/10	
Hang & Focus	10/30/10	
Painting Deck	11/2/10	
Dry Tech	11/6/10	No Actors
Costume Parade	11/7/10	None scheduled
Tech Rehearsal	11/8/10	No Costumes
Tech Rehearsal	11/7/10	Add Costumes
Dress Rehearsals	11/9-11/11	
Final Dress Rehearsals	11/12	
Opening Night	11/13	
Performances	11/14-18	
Strike	11/19/10	

REHEARSAL SPACE
        Your theatre may use the stage for rehearsals. If this is the case, find out if the set is being built there also. If it is, find out who is responsible for cleaning up after the crew has finished and how much time there is between "building" and rehearsal.

The crew will usually be responsible for cleaning up their mess. You should show up forty minutes early to do a sweep of the stage and set up for rehearsal. Even if the cast never gets down on the floor, it is still important that the space be clean.

Sometimes, the theatre will have a separate rehearsal room. Again, find out who is responsible for the upkeep of it. Maybe you will luck out and there will be a housekeeping staff person responsible for it. Then all you have to do is make sure they are doing their job. You may be the one responsible, in which case you should make a point of sweeping every day, and damp mopping twice a week. The space will get dirty just from the people walking in and out every rehearsal.

SM EXPERIENCE: I once arrived at rehearsal to discover the space wet from mopping (puddles everywhere). I dealt with it myself (no one else around), but made sure to contact the person in charge of cleaning so that it never happened again. (The puddles, that is.)

You may be using a rental space for rehearsals. They will clean it. Hurrah! You may end up being the one to locate the space. If that is the case, find out the size of the stage and then, figure out the size of the space needed for rehearsals. Rehearsal spaces come in a variety of sizes, prices and qualities.

THE THEATRE

You should find out about your theatre "as soon as possible". You may not be going into it with your actors until technical rehearsals – that is no reason for you not to get familiar with it.

Get a tour from the production manager or another contact person at the company. Try to ask questions about the space. Then, later on, go into the space by yourself. Walk around and get your bearings. See if there might be any problems (e.g. the dressing rooms are so far from the stage that a quick change will have to be done in the wings). Do this a number of times so when you come back for technical rehearsals, you will feel comfortable.

CHAPTER TWO

☑AUDITIONS/CALLBACKS

You may be asked to work on auditions. In order to get prepared for this, you need to make sure to get important information ahead of time about how the theatre usually runs them. The way auditions run will differ depending on the theatre. If there is a stage manager around who has previously worked there, you could ask them how auditions work. It is your job as a stage manager to do what ever you can to help auditions run as efficiently as possible, making sure the director gets the opportunity to see what they need to see. In most theatres the auditions will consist of two parts: auditions and callbacks.

AUDITION ORGANIZATION

The stage management job leading up to and during auditions vary from theatre to theatre. Sometimes you will be asked to organize and run them, and other times you will not be needed.

NOTICES

You may be asked to prepare an "audition notice" to be distributed around campus or town. This is a typical "who, what, where, when" flyer. Find out the following:

When and where and what time are auditions?
Who is being asked to audition? (e.g. singers)?
What do they prepare (e.g. monologue, song)?
Is there a number or email for more information?

What follows is an example of an audition flyer.

AUDITIONS!

Monday, Sept. 7th
Tuesday, Sept. 8
At 5 pm in the Sharp Theatre

Callbacks on Thursday, Sept. 10th

SOME SWEET DAY

Directed by Mary Ellen Allison

*Prepare a 2-minute monologue
AND
8 measures of a song

*Scripts are available in the library.

Any further questions, contact the Stage Manager:
Stage Manager's Name
Stage Managers' email address

Besides posting around campus/town, you can also send it to potential actors through email or facebook. It is important to get the information out so that there is a good turnout for the auditions.

PREPARING THE AUDITION SPACE
You may be asked to organize the audition space. Get there early to set up chairs and tables for the director, yourself, choreographer, etc., and a table with chair outside for your assistant. If there is a reception area, make sure there are some chairs for the actors. Locate and put up signs for the restrooms, if necessary.
You may also want to have a few chairs in the audition

room in case an auditionee wishes to use one for their audition.

RUNNING AUDITIONS

Find out if the auditionees will be signing up for a specific time slot or if it is on a "first come, first served" basis. If there are sign-ups for a specific time slot, then find out how many people the director wants to see in a given amount of time. You need to give every auditionee one minute for getting into the space, for setting up, and for leaving. If they have been asked to prepare a two-minute monologue, you will then prepare a sign-in sheet with fifteen spaces for every forty-five minutes (giving each actor 3 minutes total for the process). If the director has asked for one-minute monologues, then you would schedule fifteen people for every thirty minutes (giving each actor 2 minutes total for the process). Some directors will ask that the time be 5 minutes per person, so they may ask a few questions before and after the actor "performs" their monologue.

Once an actor signs in for a specific time slot, it is possible for them to leave the audition space and return for their scheduled audition time. If the auditionees do leave, you need to remind them to return fifteen minutes prior to their scheduled slot.

If auditions are on a first come, first served basis, without a specific time slot, then the auditionees have to sign in and wait until they are called for their audition.

SM TIP: It can feel like a circus in full swing during auditions. Actors will be coming at you to ask questions and the director will expect you to keep everything going quickly. Stay calm and make use of your assistant to deal with the actors. The director will feel as if they have been deserted if you are not close to them during the process. Stay relaxed and realize that it only lasts for a few hours and then it will be calm again.

AUDITION MATERIALS

The sign in sheet should have numbers for each person as they sign in. From that moment on, that person is connected to that number. The "audition form" that they will fill out should have this number in the upper right hand corner. If you are not using audition forms, you need to write the number in the corner of their résumé.

SIGN IN SHEET

It is important to have a sheet where the auditionees can sign in, when they arrive. On this sheet, you can note their arrival times. You can also note if there is any type of conflict. (e.g. in college, sometimes an actor will have night classes and have to leave by a specific time.) It is important that information regarding an actor's need to leave an audition at a specific time be communicated from the sign in desk to you, inside the audition space. You need to make sure the director is aware of any actors who must leave early. You can have your assistant send in notes that have a listing of the order of auditionees and their time to leave. This will alleviate the situation where the director asks an auditionee to stay and read a scene, and the actor replies, "I have to leave right now."

AUDITION SIGN IN SHEET SHOW TITLE		DATE	
Audition Number	PRINT NAME CLEARLY	TIME Arrived	Conflict with Audition
1			
2			
3			
4			
5			

AUDITION FORM

If the auditionees will not be bringing headshots and

résumés you need to be prepared for them to fill out audition forms. This should include any information that the director, music director, choreographer, or stage manager might need. That information will usually include:

Name
Phone Numbers (home, cell)
Email address
Any conflicts for rehearsals (e.g. classes, work, etc.)
A space for previous theatre experience.

The auditionee should fill out the audition form *before* they go in to perform their monologue.

AUDITION FORM
SHOW TITLE

NAME_____

Address_____ City_____ Zip_____

Home phone _____

Cell Phone_____

Email Address_____

If not cast, would you be willing to lend support in other areas of the production (e.g. crew)? _____

What would be your interest? _____

Please list any special talents or skills (dancer, musician, vocalist, tech, etc.) that would benefit the production:

Do you have any experience with stage combat and/or sports?

Theatrical Experience (Please list a few of your roles.):

Performance Dates: 4/18-4/21, 4/25-4/28

ON THE BACK, PLEASE LIST:
Work schedule
Class/School schedule

SHOW INFORMATION SHEET
 Auditionees should be aware of the dates of rehearsals, technical rehearsals, performances and strike (if they are required to attend). An information sheet with all the above information printed on it should be posted at the audition site as well as distributed to all auditionees.

 In some situations, it is necessary to have each auditionee sign and return the sheet (with a tear-off sheet of the dates) stating they have read and understand the commitment involved in the production. By doing this, later in the process, they cannot say they did not know they were needed on certain dates.

SHOW INFORMATION SHEET

First Rehearsal: Tuesday, SEPT. 3   6-11pm
Weekly Rehearsals: Monday-Friday   6-11pm
Technical Rehearsal:
 Saturday, October 12   10am-10pm
Dress Rehearsals:
 Sunday, October 13   6-11pm
 Tuesday, October 15   6-11pm
 Wednesday, October 16   6-11pm
Performances:
 Thursday, October 17   8pm (Call 6:30)
 Friday, October 18   8pm (Call 6:30)
 Saturday, October 19   8pm (Call 6:30)
Strike: Sunday, October 20
Picture Call: After the Friday, Oct. 18 Show
(Please sign the bottom, tear it off and give it to the stage manager. Keep the top part for your records.)

I, _____, have read the above listing of required dates for the show _____. I understand I need to be available for all the listed dates. By signing this form I agree to make myself available for all the dates listed.
Signed_____ Date_____

AUDITION PICTURES

It is useful to have a laptop computer or digital camera available to take headshots of all those auditioning, corresponding to their audition number. This way, the director or music director will have a reference picture when they are discussing the casting. At the end of auditions, download these pictures to a CD or use a USB flash drive, so the director can take it home, if they so desire.

EMAIL ADDRESSES

An easy way to facilitate contacting everyone that auditions is to have a laptop computer at the sign in table at auditions. Then, when each auditionee signs in, you can immediately input their email address into the computer and check with them for spelling mistakes. This will help you to dissiminate information about callbacks at the end of the audition. You will also be building a contact list for the next time you have auditions at that theatre.

AUDITION ORGANIZATION SUMMARY

1. Auditionee signs the sign in sheet.
2. Auditionee is assigned a number.
3. A stage manager inputs auditionees' email into computer.
4. A stage manager takes a picture of the auditionee.
5. Auditionee fills out audition form.
6. Auditionee reads and signs Show Information Sheet.
7. Auditionee returns audition form and any other sheets that have been requested. (e.g. class and work schedules.)
8. Auditionee is called to the holding area for their audition.

KEEPING IT RUNNING SMOOTHLY

It is important that the auditions run smoothly for everyone involved. The director does not want to be sitting in the audition room waiting for people to come in. You should have an assistant outside at the main entrance to check everyone in and organize the materials. This assistant should make sure that there is always one person in the audition room and two are "on deck", waiting to go in. If you have a second assistant, it is helpful to have that person just inside the audition room, so you can tell them when to bring the next person in to audition. Any time you can save running to get people will help the auditions run smoother.

Once the assistant has collected the audition sheets and taken audition pictures, they should send the sheets into the audition room to you. Your responsibility is to make sure that every form is in order, so that the director has the sheet to go with the person entering the room. Make sure someone is always at the front table to answer questions from those auditioning.

> SM TIP: The smooth running of auditions is an effective way to show a director that you are going to be responsible for making their experience on the show a comfortable one. If you see a problem develop. Go try to fix it.

INTRODUCTIONS

When the auditionee enters the audition room, it is customary to do introductions according to what the director prefers. You need to discuss with them how much of an introduction they would like. If you do the introductions, you will be establishing to the actors that you are the stage manager. You may introduce them by saying, "George White this is the director, Jane Smith and the music director, Joe James". At this time, to keep the introductions to a quick second, you can tell the auditionee where they should stand to perform their piece. And then you can add a "We're ready."

You should also discuss with the director how to handle the end of the audition. At the end of the audition piece, you could be the one to say, "Thank you. Callbacks will be posted…".

Sometimes the director will want to ask a question or two, but if you have established this protocol, then it is easy for them to insert a question if they need to. This gets the auditionee out of the audition room in very quick order.

CALLBACK ORGANIZATION

Yet again, every theatre and director has their own idea about how to organize and run callbacks.

SCHEDULING

This may be done by the director, but sometimes, you are asked to organize the callbacks. The director might want each actor for 10 minutes, or a small group of actors for a limited time (e.g. 30 minutes). This "group" might be all the actors for a certain character, or 2-3 actors for 2-3 different characters that are in scenes together. Your job is to try to organize the callbacks so the director sees what they need to see in order to cast the show.

Once the callbacks are scheduled it is your job to get the appropriate information to those that are called back.

NOTIFYING AUDITIONEES

You must now notify all those that are called back what time to be at the audition space and what to prepare. You prepared an email list as the auditionees signed in for their audition. Depending on the director, you can send the callback notice to everyone who auditioned, or only to those who are called back. The director may choose to write a note to those who are not called back to thank them for their time. Or you may send the callback schedule to everyone that auditioned. The callback schedule should also be posted on the theatre callboard, so those that do not check their email regularly will have a way of being told about callbacks.

DISTRIBUTION OF INFORMATION

Find a way to get scenes ("sides") to those that will be coming for the callbacks. If you are in a college situation, you might find a central location (e.g. the secretary's office or the green room) where the actors can come to pick up their scenes. You might be able to email them the scenes if the play is in a computer document.

The following are some of the materials that you may need to get to the actors.

CHARACTER DESCRIPTIONS

The director may ask you to distribute character descriptions to those that are called back. You are not responsible for writing the descriptions. The director will give them to you. They are useful to the actors, as they may not have had an opportunity to read the script.

SIDES/SCENES

Prior to auditions, the director will give you a list of scenes to be used for callbacks. You need to verify with them how many actors they anticipate calling back for each character. Then, make copies of each scene (with two extras for each scene). Every scene should be clearly marked as to which character the actor should be reading. For every actor called back, you can make a little package of the specific scenes that person will be asked to read.

If you happen to be using whole scripts, you need to make sure they are numbered and assigned to specific actors. That way, when auditions are over, you will have a way of knowing who to contact if a script is missing.

RUNNING CALLBACKS

As with the first day of auditions, an assistant should be at the front desk, outside the audition room, to "check in" those arriving for the callbacks. They should make sure the actors have the correct sides. They can also let the actors know if callbacks are running late.

It is your job to expedite the entire process. If the stage manager is organized and running things properly, it will run smoothly for all involved.

It does not hurt to be nice. Just a kind word or two makes the auditionees feel a lot better. Remember, there are a lot of them. When an actor is called in, you can introduce yourself. You can talk to them as you walk them in and out. It does not add time to the process and it establishes you as the stage manager in charge. Some of them will be working with you shortly. You may not remember them all, but they will remember you.

You or your assistant may be asked to serve as a "reader" for auditions or callbacks. A "reader" is someone who reads the lines of the other characters in the scene the auditionee is using. Readers allow the director to focus on one person. Make sure the reader is sitting adjacent to the audition area. They should be parallel to the stage, so that they are facing both the actor and the director. The reader should have a music stand on which to place their script. Make sure they have the appropriate sides. If the director asks for the reader to stand on the stage, remember that the focus is on the person auditioning, so the reader should stand in a position that does not draw emphasis away from the auditionee. (The reader should stand a little downstage of the auditionee.)

If the director asks to see a group of people, e.g. six actors from 4-4:30pm, etc., then you must do your best to keep the pace up. Don't waste time. Know exactly who they want to see in what order and have the next group or person waiting "on deck". Your communication skills are important here. The director may say, "I want Joe and Linda with Scene 2 and then Beba and John with Scene 3". In this situation, have Beba and John waiting "on deck" so the moment the director is finished with Joe and Linda, Beba and John can be ushered in. (Sometimes, the director wants a moment to make notes before the next group enters.) The director should never have to wait for the stage managers to find an actor. It is important to find out if the director is finished with an actor, and then, let the actor know they may leave.

> SM TIP: Do your best to keep the auditions flowing smoothly. Don't forget breaks for the director. Keep your best face on and "anticipate" as much as you can.

CAST LIST

Once the director has chosen a cast, you can make a listing of the actor's and their characters. This list can be emailed to those who auditioned and posted on the callboard.

CHAPTER THREE

☑REHEARSAL SCHEDULES

Putting together a rehearsal schedule is probably the most complicated aspect of stage managing. You will often be working around conflicts that the actors may have (e.g. work) and you will be trying to give the director everything they need. In addition, you might be called on to organize multiple rehearsals that occur simultaneously.

If you are working in a situation where the entire cast is being paid a living wage for their work on the production, then the director will probably rehearse the play from the beginning to the end, in chronological order, and every one in the cast will be at every rehearsal the entire time. Then the schedule will depend on what the director wants to accomplish in that rehearsal.

If you are responsible for organizing the rehearsal schedule, the first thing you need to do is find out from the director how many days they want to spend "blocking the play". It may be that there will be two weeks of rehearsal to block the play be-fore a first run through. Do not assume that the director will block the whole play before returning to work on scenes. In order to keep it simple, I will organize the schedules in this chapter for a simple non-musical play.

CONFLICTS

In many situations, the cast will have work or class schedules that conflict with rehearsal and that you will have to schedule around. Keep it simple. The first thing to do is make a

list of all the actors and their scheduling conflicts for each rehearsal. Make sure you note the hours the actor is *not* available
for each day of the rehearsal schedule (include travel time, if
necessary).

Once you have a list of all the actors' conflicts, you can
summarize them into a concise sheet that only shows the actors
that have conflicts and the times they are unavailable.

ACTOR CONFLICTS				
SHOW TITLE				

	MON.	TUES.	WED.	THURS.	FRI.
John	NONE	NONE	NONE	NONE	NONE
Beth	NONE	NONE	7-9:30	NONE	NONE
Richard	6-11:00	NONE	6-8:30	NONE	NONE
Albert	NONE	NONE	NONE	6-11:00	NONE
Michele	6-11:00	NONE	NONE	NONE	NONE

By putting all of the conflicts on one sheet, it will be
easier to determine the actual schedule.

DAILY CONFLICTS				Date
SHOW TITLE				

Monday	Tuesday	Wednesday	Thursday	Friday
6-11 Richard Michele	6-11 NONE	6-8:30 Richard 7-9:30 Elizabeth	6-11 Albert	6-11 NONE

MEET WITH THE DIRECTOR

At this time, take your conflict sheet and make an appointment to meet with the director to talk about the rehearsal schedule. You may use the conflict sheet to determine what times the director would like to have rehearsals, or they may have decided this prior to the auditions. At this meeting, you will make sure you have all the pertinent information to be included in the rehearsal schedule for the actors. This rehearsal schedule will have all the dates for rehearsals, technical rehearsals and performances. It is important that you note clearly on the schedule if there are any rehearsals scheduled on days or at times that are not *usual* rehearsal days/times. If the director chooses to do the rehearsal schedule, make sure to give them all the information needed regarding conflicts. Ask if they want you to proof it before giving it out to the actors. In that way, you can look it for any conflicts that they may have missed.

SM TIP: As a novice stage manager, you may not be asked to actually determine the rehearsal schedule. Many directors, in that situation, will want to organize their own schedule. You should try to be part of the process so you know *what* is happening *when*, and can then watch for any problems with conflicts or times.

REHEARSAL SCHEDULE

Type the rehearsal schedule on a calendar so that the actors can see the big picture as far as the production is concerned. The rehearsal schedule is the overview of the entire process of rehearsals. It is important to make sure to include all the technical rehearsals and at least opening night. (You can get these dates from your production calendar). Be specific with the times of rehearsals, as it will help the actors to clarify when they are needed through the entire process. Once the rehearsal schedule is complete, you will then make a weekly schedule that has much more detail regarding call times and scene work.

Below is a rehearsal schedule for a show with six weeks of rehearsal. There will be five nights of rehearsal and each night the rehearsal will run from 6-11 o'clock. There is one weekend of "technical rehearsals" followed by three "dress rehearsals". The show runs from Wednesday through Sunday with "strike" following the show on Sunday.

SEPTEMBER/OCTOBER REHEARSAL SCHEDULE *SOME SWEET DAY*					Date	
Sun.	Mon.	Tues.	Wed.	Thurs.	Fri.	Sat.
1	2	3 Reh. 6-11	4 Reh. 6-11	5 Reh. 6-11	6 Reh. 6-11	7
8	9 Reh. 6-11	10 Reh. 6-11	11 Reh. 6-11	12 Reh. 6-11	13 Reh. 6-11	14
15	16 Reh. 6-11	17 Reh. 6-11	18 Reh. 6-11	19 Reh. 6-11	20 Reh. 6-11	21
22	23 Reh. 6-11	24 Reh. 6-11	25 Reh. 6-11	26 Reh. 6-11	27 Reh. 6-11	28
29	30 Reh. 6-11	1 Reh. 6-11	2 Reh. 6-11	3 Reh. 6-11	4 Reh. 6-11	5
6	7 Reh. 6-11	8 Reh. 6-11	9 Reh. 6-11	10 Reh. 6-11	11 Dry Tech 6-11	12 Tech 10-10
13 Tech 10-10	14 Dress 6-11	15 Dress 6-11	16 OPEN 8:00	17 Show 8:00	18 Show 8:00	19 Show 8:00
20 Show 3:00	21	22	23	24	25	26

DAILY SCHEDULE

The director may say that all actors have to be at all rehearsals except for when they have noted conflicts. In this case, you notify the actors that they will be at *all* rehearsals at *all* times. Obviously, this is the easiest to schedule.

Most likely, the director will want to give the actors a daily rehearsal schedule that is posted (and distributed) at the end of one day's rehearsal for the next day's rehearsal. In this schedule, you will give the actors an idea of the plan for the next day. Any special aspects of the rehearsal should be noted.

DAILY REHEARSAL SCHEDULE
SHOW TITLE
THURSDAY, APRIL 12

6-8:00　Everyone (Work End of Show)

8:00　Everyone (Run Through Off Book for Designers)

11:00　End of Rehearsal

WEEKLY SCHEDULE

At your meeting with the director, you will also find out how they want to organize their weekly schedule of rehearsals. The following are several possible scenarios that you might encounter.

SCENARIO ONE:

The director says they would like to give the actors some free time during the week and would like to schedule "groups" of actors for different times. For example, if you are doing *Romeo and Juliet* you could first work with Romeo and Juliet for a couple of hours, and then the remainder of the rehearsal period with Romeo, Mercutio, Benvolio, Tybalt and the rest of "the guys". Another time you may work with Lord and Lady Capulet, the Nurse, Peter and Juliet for a few hours and then work with Romeo, Juliet and the Priest. The remaining nights the whole cast is called. Use your conflicts sheet to organize the nights the director could have each of the groups for rehearsal.

Then, for each week you would generate a weekly rehearsal schedule that would inform the actors what specific scenes you will work. The director may give you a list at the end of each week with the following week's detailed schedule for you to distribute to the cast. Or they may give you a list of scenes and ask that you organize the week's schedule.

SM TIP: Having group rehearsals are a very effective way to deal with weekly conflicts. The actors know exactly which nights and times they are called weeks ahead. Make sure to inform them that once you are getting near the technical rehearsals, the schedule may change.

SCENARIO TWO:

The director says he wants to work whatever scenes work with the actor's conflicts. In this scenario, there is no real chronological order to working through the play (although, some nights you will work the scheduled scenes chronologically). The first thing you must do is figure out how much time to allocate to each scene.

TIME ALLOCATION

It is possible to look at a schedule as a mathematical equation. It is a very simple equation and goes like this: the number of pages in the script ÷ by the number of hours to accomplish the task = the number of pages that need to be scheduled per hour. In other words, if the script is 100 pages long, and your director wants to finish blocking it in 5 days, with rehearsal lasting 4 hours per day, then the equation would be: 100 pages ÷ 20 hours (5 days X 4 hours) = 5 pages per hour.

The next step is to look at each scene and how long it is. If the scene is 5 pages in length, you schedule it for 1 hour. If it is 3 pages long, 30 minutes. Figure out when there need to be breaks for the actors and director. You may schedule a 6-page scene for 1 hour and a 4-page scene for 1 hour, making a note that there will be a break after the 6-page scene. This is not perfect, but works very well with "straight plays". (Musicals are another problem that I will talk about in a separate chapter.) At this point, note on the "scene breakdown" how many pages there are for each scene. You have determined how much time is going to be allotted to each scene and you know what the conflicts are going to be. Now it is time to start putting the schedule together.

> SM EXPERIENCE: I "discovered" this formula a long time ago while working my first show in New York. If doing Shakespeare, figure it out using the total number of lines in the play and the number of lines per hour of rehearsal. It is an approximation, but I have used it successfully for years.

For the purposes of this exercise I will generate a scene breakdown for a hypothetical show. The following steps will relate to this breakdown and not *Some Sweet Day*.

SCENE BREAKDOWN ACT ONE SHOW TITLE									
Scene	1	2	3	4	5	6	7	8	9
Page numbers	2	14	22	32	38	41	57	68	83
# of pages	12	8	10	6	4	16	11	15	8
John	X	X	X	X		X		X	X
Beth	X	X	X		X	X	X		
Richard		X		X	X		X		
Albert			X	X			X	X	
Michelle								X	X

ORGANIZING THE SCHEDULE

For a lot of stage managers, this is the hardest part of the job. It is definitely one of the most complicated. But others may find it easy. Don't get discouraged by the math involved. It is simple and I will talk you through it step by step.

For our example assume the following: the director asks you to schedule blocking rehearsals for all scenes in Act I in the first week of rehearsal.

WEEK ONE

STEP ONE:

Utilizing your conflict schedule, make a list of all the scenes that you could possibly rehearse at every rehearsal (note both act and scene numbers). There will be some repetition, but don't worry about that at this time.

POSSIBLE SCENES SHOW TITLE			Date	
Monday	Tuesday	Wednesday	Thursday	Friday
I/1, I/3, I/5	All Scenes	I/8, I/9	I/1, I/2, I/3, I/6, I/9	All Scenes
		Before 7:00- I/1, I/3, I/6		
		After 8:30- I/3, I/4		
		After 9:30- All Scenes		

STEP TWO:

Figure out (using the mathematical formula) how much time you need to allocate for each scene. For purposes of this chapter, let us say the director wants to block Act I in the first week.

Equation: The number of days of rehearsal, times the number of hours per day, will equal the total number of possible rehearsal hours. Then, you take the total number of pages to cover and divide that by the total number of rehearsal hours, which will equal the number of pages you need to schedule per hour of rehearsal.

OR

\# Days of rehearsal X # Hours/day = Total Rehearsal Hours

Total Pages -:- Total Rehearsal Hours = Pages per Hour

For our example, then, it would be:

5 days X 5 hours/day = 25 total hours each week

Total Script Pages = 90

90 Divided by 25 = 3.6 pages per hour

To simplify, I would round it to 3.5 pages per hour.

STEP THREE:

Determine how many hours of rehearsal you need for each scene, rounding the time up or down to the nearest 15 minutes.

Equation: The number of pages in each scene divided by the number of pages per hour will equal the number of hours you should assign to that scene.

OR

\# pages in scene -:- # pages/hour = # hrs. for scene

For our example, it would be:

Scene 1 = 12 pages; 12 ÷ 3.5 = 3.4 hours, round down to 3.25

Scene 2 = 8 pages; 8 ÷ 3.5 = 2.3 hours, round down to 2.25

Scene 3 = 10 pages; 10 ÷ 3.5 = 2.9 hours, round up to 3.0

Scene 4 = 6 pages; 6 ÷ 3.5 = 1.7 hours, round down to 1.5

Scene 5 = 4 pages; 4 ÷ 3.5 = 1.14 hours, round down to 1.0

Scene 6 = 16 pages; 16 ÷ 3.5 = 4.6 hours, round down to 4.5

Scene 7 = 11 pages; 11 ÷ 3.5 = 3.14 hours, round down to 3.0

Scene 8 = 15 pages; 15 ÷ 3.5 = 4.3 hours, round down to 4.25

Scene 9 = 8 pages; 8 ÷ 3.5 = 2.3 hours, round down to 2.25

STEP FOUR:

At this point add up the number of hours you have calculated for each scene to get a total number of hours needed to cover the whole act. If it does not add up to the total number of hours you have to rehearse, then, you need to alter the number of hours for each scene a little to make it work out. For instance, I could have initially rounded the time for Scene 1 from 3.4 UP to 3.5 (three and a half hours). Instead I rounded it DOWN to 3.25 (3 hours 15 minutes) in order to make it work within the time alotted for the rehearsals.

STEP FIVE:

Now get out the "possible scenes" sheet. Because Wednesday night is the most complicated, start with that.

For our example:

Wednesday: Scenes 8 & 9 can be done at any time that night. The rehearsal hours needed add up to 6 hours 30 minutes but the scheduled rehearsal time is only 5 hours long. So you could do "I/8" (Act I, Scene 8) for 4 hours 15 minutes, leaving you 45 minutes for another scene. Instead of trying to figure out which scene to do in these 45 minutes, for now, move to the next night.

Monday: only 3 scenes can be done that night. Start with I/1 and assign it the 3 hours 15 minutes it requires. With the remaining 1 hour 45 minutes, you could start I/3. I/3 needs 3 hours total, so you have to give it 1 hour 15 minutes another night.

Tuesday: Start by assigning 1 hour 15 minutes to I/3. Then move on to another night because on Tuesday, there are no conflicts and any scene may be rehearsed.

Thursday: I/1 has already been assigned a time. Give I/2, 2 hours 15 minutes. I/3 has already been assigned a time. Give I/6 the remaining 2 hours 45 minutes. That fills the night up and leaves you with I/6 needing 1 hour and 45 minutes to finish. Because you started I/6 on Thursday, you can put it into Friday to finish it.

Friday: I/6 for 1 hour 45 minutes.

Monday	Tuesday	Wednesday	Thursday	Friday
I/1: 3¼ hour	I/3: 1¼ hour	I/8: 4¼ hour	I/2: 2¼ hour	I/6: 1¾ hour
I/3: 1¾ hour			I/6: 2¾ hour	

STEP SIX:

At this point look at your schedule to see how much time is left in each rehearsal block and what scenes are left to be inserted into the schedule.

For our example:

Scenes done:

I/1, I/2, I/3, I/6, and I/ 8

Scenes not started:

I/4 (1 hour 30 minutes)

I/5 (1 hour)

I/7 (3 hours)

I/9 (2 hours 15 minutes)

Hours left for each night of rehearsal:

Monday	0 hours
Tuesday	3 hours 45 minutes
Wednesday	45 minutes
Thursday	0 hours
Friday	3 hours 15 minutes

STEP SEVEN:

Now it is time to figure out where to assign the remaining scenes.

For our example:

Tuesday: You have 3 hours 45 minutes left and scenes I/4 and I/9 add up to 3 hours 45 minutes. Assign them to Tuesday.

Wednesday: Because you only have 45 minutes left, assign I/7 to it, so that you can get a start on this longer scene.

Friday: Assign the remaining 2 hours 15 minutes of I/7, and I/5 for 1 hour.

You have now assigned each scene to a rehearsal night. Now comes the fun part: trying to make all of what you have done work each night.

| POSSIBLE SCHEDULE ASSIGNMENTS   Date | | | | |
| SHOW TITLE | | | | |

Monday	Tuesday	Wednesday	Thursday	Friday
I/1: 3¼ hour	I/3: 1¼ hour	I/8: 4¼ hour	I/2: 2¼ hour	I/6: 1¾ hour
I/3: 1¾ hour	I/4: 1½ hour	I/7: ¾ hour	I/6: 2¾ hour	I/7: 2¼ hour
	I/9: 2¼ hour			I/5: 1 hour

STEP EIGHT:

The last step is to look at the schedule and the order of the scenes and make sure they make sense. On Monday and Tuesday, the scenes are in sequence. On Wednesday, they are not in sequence, but one actor has a conflict in the early evening, so I/7 has to be scheduled at the end. Thursday, the scenes are in sequence as well. On Friday, you have the entire cast so why not start with I/5, then go to I/6 and end with I/7? That way, there will be some continuity.

Now it is time to put it on paper as a rehearsal schedule to be given to the director for their approval. If there are no problems with the schedule then it is ready to distribute to the cast. It needs to be clear and concise. Make sure it includes the day and date for each rehearsal. Then, break down each rehearsal day into assigned times, i.e. the scenes that will be worked on and the actors required for those scenes. This is very important, as it will help the actors determine when they are called and what scene to have prepared.

REHEARSAL SCHEDULE		Date
WEEK OF APRIL 12 TO APRIL 16		
SHOW TITLE		

MONDAY, APRIL 12

6:00	I/1	John, Beth (Actors)
9:15	I/3	John, Beth

TUESDAY, APRIL 13

6:00	I/3	John, Beth
7:15	I/4	John, Richard, Albert
8:45	I/9	John, Michelle

WEDNESDAY, APRIL 14

6:00	I/8	John, Albert, Michele
10:15	I/7	Beth, Richard, Albert

THURSDAY, APRIL 15

6:00	I/2	John, Beth, Richard
8:15	I/6	John, Beth

FRIDAY, APRIL 16

6:00	I/5	Beth, Richard, Albert
7:00	I/6	John, Beth
8:45	I/7	Beth, Richard, Albert

When you distribute a schedule for the following week, you could change the color of the paper it is printed on, to differentiate it from other weeks.

You have now organized the first week of the rehearsal and scheduled every scene in Act One. Suppose the following week the director wants to revisit Act One scenes but start on Act Two as well and they give you a list of the first five scenes in Act Two.

SM TIP: Be aware that a small adjustment to the schedule could have rippling effects. If the director says to change one thing, check conflicts and the rest of the schedule to make sure the "small" change hasn't blown the whole schedule out of whack.

WEEK TWO

You can follow the same basic procedures as with week one. Most directors will not require as much time working on scenes as they did to block them. Ask the director how much time they want to spend working each scene. Then looking at the schedule you made for Act One, leave those scenes on the same days because you know the conflicts are the same. Cut down the time scheduled for those individual scenes to the amount of time the director wants. This will tell you how much time you will have left on each night of rehearsal to schedule the new scenes. Then you follow the same process that you did for week one only for a smaller amount of time and fewer scenes.

SM TIP: Working out a rehearsal schedule is a grueling process. Often, you will work for hours, realize you missed a scene, and have to start all over again. Or, you work for hours and the director says, "It doesn't work for me." Or, you get the OK from the director and when you hand them out to the actors, one of them says, "I forgot to tell you that I have a doctor's appointment on Tuesday, and can't make it to rehearsal until 7:00." Often, you will have to re-work a schedule several times before it is completed. Don't despair. It is one of the jobs that a stage manager does that looks simple, yet is very time consuming.

WEEK THREE

During week three the director could tell you that they want to work Act One again, revisit the first five scenes of Act Two, and block the remaining five scenes. Follow the same procedure you did for week two. Adjust the amount of time for Act One and the first five scenes of Act Two. This will give you the time you have left to work the remaining scenes.

This is a long and laborious process. It is like a three dimensional puzzle where you are working with many schedules of actors and specific needs of the director. Make sure to run any schedules past the director before giving them to the actors.

You have now worked through organizing a relatively simple rehearsal schedule. I say *relatively*, because there are actually no simple rehearsal schedules. Each show has its own problems as far as scheduling is concerned. All I hope to do is give you a good start.

MULTIPLE/SIMULTANEOUS REHEARSALS

On some shows (e.g. musicals) there will be rehearsals with the music director and the choreographer. Sometimes these multiple rehearsals are scheduled at different times than the rehearsals with the director. At other times multiple rehearsals will happen simultaneously. Perhaps there are combat or music or dialect needs in the show and someone will be working with some members of the cast while the director is working with others. I have no formula for this situation. It is like a big puzzle for which you must figure out how to make the pieces fit when they aren't the correct shapes that you need. A musical might have music, dance and acting rehearsals while an outdoor drama may have acting, combat, firearms, and equestrian rehearsals all happening simultaneously.

The easiest way to figure out how to schedule a multiple rehearsal is to use the scene breakdown. Then you ask the director and whoever is running the other rehearsal how much time they need for each scene, actor or musical number.

For our purposes, let us say that you have combat and equestrian work, in addition to the acting. Go to the director, the combat director, and the head equestrian. Find out *what* they would like to rehearse and for *how long* they would like to rehearse. Write their requests down. For the following example, there are five actors (A, B, C, D, & E) and the rest of the company is called when it says "all". The following are their requests for rehearsal time.

Acting:		
	Actors A & B	1 hour
	Actors A & E	1 hour
	Actors C & D	1 hour
	Actors B & C	1 hour
	All actors	1 hour
	All (except C & D)	1 hour

Combat: All (exc. A, B, C, D & E) 1 hour
          A & B   1 hour
          C & D   1 hour
Equestrian: All riders (exc. A, B, C & D) 1 hour
          A & E   1 hour
          C, D & E   1 hour

After gathering this information, I would start with the director and acting rehearsals. Then, I would see what we could do opposite those rehearsals. The first thing that I note is that it is possible to have three rehearsals going on at the same time. While the director is working with A & B, the equestrian could be with C & D & E, and the fight director could have all the combatants (except A, B, C, D & E).

	ACTING	COMBAT	HORSE
1 hr	A & B	All (exc: A,B,C,D,E)	C, D & E

If there are enough rehearsal spaces I would suggest this to all concerned. Then as I work through the rest of the schedule I see the following works opposite each other.

	ACTING	COMBAT	HORSE
1 hr	A & E		All (exc: A,B,C&D)
1 hr	C & D	A & B	
1 hr	B & C		A & E
1 hr	All (exc: C & D)	C & D	
1 hr	All		

So we have a six-hour rehearsal period with two or three rehearsals going on.

There is no tried and true way to organize multiple rehearsals. You will spend many hours writing down possible schedules to realize that one does not work. Then, when you start over, it turns out to work except for one time slot. Often you have to go to one of the participants, ask if they could take a *shorter time* for the next rehearsal, and then a *longer one* the following day. If everyone works together it is possible to work out. Gently remind everyone, they have to stick to the schedule, or it throws the whole day off for everyone. It is necessary to communicate effectively with all the people in charge of these aspects. Everyone needs to keep in mind the necessity to give and take, in order to organize simultaneous rehearsals.

MULTIPLE REHEARSAL SPACES

You need to make sure when you have multiple rehearsals that there is an appropriate second space and that it is reserved for the times that it is needed for rehearsal. If it is table work or dialect work it may be that the dressing room or green room is a viable space. Even the lobby of the theatre can be used, if necessary.

PART TWO

REHEARSAL PROCESS

CHAPTER FOUR

☑FIRST REHEARSALS

Putting together a show is a long process and the first rehearsal is just the beginning. As you head into it, remember to relax. Even if you have forgotten to do something, stay calm.

REHEARSAL SPACE

It is imperative that you find out where your rehearsals will be held and that you see the space prior to the first rehearsal. As with auditions, you may be in a rented space, which means you do not need to worry about the upkeep, but you do have to make sure there are tables and chairs (set up appropriately).

CALLBOARD

If there is not already a callboard, you need to establish a place in your rehearsal hall where you will post information. Post only important information, so the cast knows not to overlook anything that is on it. Any written notices generated should be posted on it. The following are some items that are usually found there.

Company Rules
Rehearsal Schedule
Costume Fitting Schedule
Production Meeting Schedules
Interesting Info. (e.g. menus from local restaurants)
Equity information (if it is an equity show)
Sign in Sheet

CONTACT SHEET

For the first rehearsal, you must create a contact sheet to distribute to every member of the company. Double check to make sure that everyone's information is correct. This contact sheet does not have to include the creative staff, if they are not working directly with the cast.

COMPANY CONTACT SHEET *SOME SWEET DAY*		Date
Harry Alston (Director)	Email address	(cell) 123-456-7890
John Combes (Stage Mgr.)	Email address	(cell) 234-567-8910
Jerry Lanham (Music Director)	Email address	(cell) 345-678-9101
S. Temple (Choreographer)	Email address	(cell) 456-789-1011
Debbie Armstrong (Clea)	Email address	(cell) 567-891-0111
Chelsea Cole (Sarah Jane)	Email address	(cell) 678-910-1112
Tom David (Isaac)	Email address	(cell) 789-101-1121
Nick Dobney (Buddy)	Email address	(cell) 891-011-1213
Ashley Field (Mae)	Email address	(home) 910-111-2131
Hanna Gentry (Child)	Email address	(cell) 101-112-1314

THE FIRST REHEARSAL

As stated in the previous chapter, what needs to be accomplished at the first rehearsal should be discussed with the director. The cast and staff will usually sit together for a read through and to introduce themselves. There may be one table large enough for the whole group. If not, you will need to put several tables together in a way no one is sitting in a second row. However, if your cast is very large, you may need to have seats in a second row, or a large circle without tables instead. You should find out if the director wants the actors to sit in assigned seats or sit wherever they choose. Sometimes they will prefer actors to sit near those characters that they will be interacting with the most during the show.

The director will have an idea of what they want to accomplish during this rehearsal. If they want a "meet and greet" session at the beginning, complete with snacks and drinks, then you will probably be responsible for getting the goodies and setting them up on tables. Make sure to ask about money for this expense. Some times the director will have a small amount of cash for these purposes. You should not be expected to pay for them.

> SM TIP: At this rehearsal, you should collect the actor's bios and headshots, or let them know the date by which these will be needed.

CALLS

The first rehearsal is a good time to remind the actors that rehearsal begins at the posted start time. They should be prepared to start working at that time, and not be just arriving, still needing to put down their things, find their script, hang their coat, etc.

You should arrive at least thirty minutes prior to the posted call. This way you have time to sweep the stage—even if it looks clean. You can also set up the set and prop rehearsal pieces for the first scene that is to be rehearsed, and then afterward get organize for the rest of the rehearsal.

THE FIRST READ THROUGH

The first "read through" is usually done without any breaks, except for a short one at "intermission", if the play is a full-length one. The director usually informs the actors that any questions should be held until the end so that you, the stage manager, can get an accurate timing of each act. You should know ahead of time how they wish the read through to proceed: How much of the stage directions would the director like you to read out loud? Do they want you to read out loud every "John enters"? Or do they want you to only read the information at the beginning of each scene like "Lights up in the church"? Whichever it is, the actors need to be informed before the read through so they'll know what to expect in terms of when it is their turn to read.

Reading the stage directions should be done in a strong, clear voice. Make sure all the actors can hear you. You may also be "making" the sound cues during this read through, whenever appropriate. (e.g. knocking on the table for a knock at the door.) The director may or may not be following the reading in their script. Don't expect them to do the sounds.

> SM TIP: At the first rehearsal, you are possibly meeting the cast for the first time. It is important that you make a good impression. Stay calm and collected. Make sure you have enough copies of all the paperwork (e.g. contact sheet, rehearsal schedule) for each of the company mem-bers. Be prepared. Although the director is in charge, it is essential that the company realize that you are the stage manager and that you are pro-active in the work that you must perform.

TIMING OF FIRST READ THROUGH

It will be helpful to the director if you keep a "timing sheet" from the very first read through. This sheet should note the running time of the read through and be broken down into your rehearsal scenes and acts. Every time you have a run through, you should note the date of the rehearsal, the running time of the act, each scene, as well as the total for the play. To have a chart like this is very informative as your rehearsals progress. You can see how much time is being added with set, costume and lighting changes.

What follows is a sample of an Act One timing sheet. Continue in the same manner with Act Two and have a row at the bottom of the page for a running total of the play's time.

TIMING SHEET *SOME SWEET DAY*					
	4/2 Read Thru	4/15 Run Thru			
Scene 1	15:15				
Scene 2	3:45				
Scene 3	8:30				
Scene 4	5:20				
Scene 5					
Scene 6					
Scene 7					
Scene 8					
Scene 9					
Scene 10					
ACT I Total					

SIGN IN SHEET

The call board will also be used as a place for cast members to sign in. It is important to establish this routine: they will need to do it for performances as well. Start using the sign in sheet at the second rehearsal. A sheet of paper with each cast member's name, and spaces for them to initial under the correct date/day/time will do. This way, right before rehearsal starts, you can check it and let the director know if anybody is absent or late.

	Tues. 4/12	Wed. 4/13	Thur. 4/14	Sat. 4/16 10:00	Sat. 4/16 2:00
Chelsea Cole					
Tom David					
Nick Dobney					
Ashley Field					
Hanna Gentry					

SIGN IN SHEET
SOME SWEET DAY
WEEK OF 4/12-4/15

SUBSEQUENT REHEARSALS

Some directors will spend the first few rehearsals doing table work. This is where the actors and director sit around a table working on the script to make sure they all understand what is being said in the play and have the same interpretation. Other directors will want to get the show "on its feet" quickly and will start blocking at the second rehearsal. You have to be ready for both kinds of directors. At your meeting concerning the rehearsal schedule, the director should have told you what they are going to do at all subsequent rehearsals. For the rest of this chapter we will assume the director wants to skip the table work and start putting the show on its feet.

WORK STATION

You need to set up a table as a work station for yourself, the director and your assistants. Sometimes, the director will want a table to themselves so that you will not be getting into each other's way. Put the director where they want to be. Usually, it is in the center of the "audience" area. The stage management table should be positioned where nobody will be crossing the director's line of sight if one of you has to get up to leave or go backstage during rehearsal.

Make sure there is enough space for you to spread out

without getting into the director's way while still close enough to communicate with them throughout the rehearsal.

SWEEPING

I know it sounds silly, but there really is a right way and a wrong way to sweep a stage. First, you need to make sure you have a good broom: one that does not leave a thin layer of dust where you have just swept. You must sweep in small strokes, always overlapping strokes and never just pushing the broom all the way across the floor. After sweeping the "dust" into one or two piles, sweep it into a dust pan and throw it away: do not ever leave a pile of dirt sitting off to the side somewhere. Someone will walk through it and track it all over the space. Even if the space looks "clean", sweep it again before every rehearsal. You never know when an actor will get down on the floor or go barefoot. Better safe than sorry.

SEATING FOR CAST MEMBERS

If there is no green room, figure out the best area for actors to "hang out" while they are not actively involved with the rehearsal. Make sure the area has ample space for them to put their bags and sit, without having to cross in front of the director and stage managers.

During a run through, this will change. You will need to set up chairs in the back stage right and left areas so the actors will not have to walk through the stage area to get to their belongings.

REHEARSAL PROPS

It is your job to find things for the actors to use during rehearsals that are suitable substitutes for props that will be used in the show. They do not have to be the actual props or even look like them, but something is needed for every single prop. Make sure to tell the actors where the rehearsal props are located, and which thing is substituting for which prop, as they may not recognize them. You can take time at this point to tape a grid (using masking tape) on the top of a table that you will use as the "prop table" backstage during performances. This way, once you move into the theatre, they will be comfortable with finding their props on the table.

You should start finding rehearsal props before rehearsals begin. They should be ready by the second rehearsal at the latest. Once the actors start to work without their scripts, they will be needing props in their hands. It is very frustrating for a director to have to ask the stage manager to get rehearsal props together. Anticipate the need and do it ahead of time.

> SM TIP: In the professional theatre, it is understood that once a scene is blocked, the next time it is worked, the actor is "off book" for it. That is why it is important to have rehearsal props from the beginning.

TAPING THE FLOOR

The set designer or technical director should give you a complete floor plan prior to your first rehearsal. A floor plan of a set design will give you a bird's eye view of the setting. It is then your job to tape the rehearsal floor to the dimensions of the floor plan. You will tape out doors, walls, steps, platforms, etc. Any part of the setting that will affect an actor's movement on or off the stage should be shown on the floor of the rehearsal space. The cast can see the layout of the setting as the set designer describes it during the first meeting.

> SM TIP: The designer or the technical director may help you tape out the set in your rehearsal space. You do not have to tape out the entire floor plan, and the taping does not have to be perfect (the actors will walk all over the lines anyway).

Tape out the floor plan on the floor of the rehearsal hall with "spike tape". You must not use masking tape. It will disintegrate and take you hours to get off the floor, and it might pull up the paint. You should also not use gaffers or duct tape (for the same reasons). Spike tape is a tape that is made of cloth and is half an inch wide; it comes in many colors. If you type, "spike tape" into your search engine on the Internet, entries come up for ordering over the net, or addresses of specialty stores in your area where it is available. The theatre should have different colors of spike tape in stock.

Most designers use 1/2 inch scale (although some have been know to use a 1/4 inch scale). The scale will be noted in the bottom right hand corner of the floor plan. If the scale on the floor plan says ½"=1'0" this means 1/2 inch on the floor plan is equal to 1 foot on the set. If the scale is ¼"=1'0", then ¼" on a ruler is equal to one foot on the set and so on. If you have an architect's scale ruler, it is relatively simple to measure all the pieces on the floor plan that need to be taped. If you do not have an architect's scale ruler, you can use a 12 inch ruler. (If you would like to learn how to use an architect's scale ruler, the internet has several sites that will talk you through the steps).

Simple math will allow you to figure out the lengths and sizes of everything on the floor plan. Using a standard ruler, when the floor plan is in a ½ inch scale, a wall that is 3 inches long (on the floor plan) will be 6 feet on the set (If you break 3 inches into ½ inch parts, there will be 6 of them).

You may be measuring something that is less than ½ inch on the floor plan, e.g. a step. On a ½" scale, every ¼ inch would be equal to 6 inches on the set. Then 1/8 inch on the floor plan would be equal to 3 inches on the set. So if something is 3/8 inches on the floor plan, it would be 9 inches on the set.

The designer should have put a "center line" on the drawing. If they have not, you need to measure the distance between the outside walls of the stage area and then divide the measurement in half to find the exact center of the stage. Then, using a 90 degree angle, mark a line through the center of the set. You will also need to mark a line on the floor plan (perpendicular to the center line) that extends across the front of the stage. This will give you intersecting lines to enable you to figure out where a set piece (e.g. wall, step, window) is positioned on the stage. You will use these lines to determine the distance from the intersection point (center point A) of the stage.

For our process, the following set up will guide you.

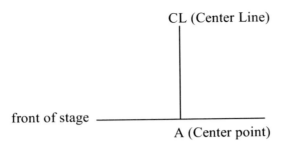

To make the taping easier for yourself, you can use four 25 foot long measuring tapes (standard retractable tapes that can be found at any home supply or hardware store).

PRELIMINARY STEPS TO TAPING THE FLOOR
1) Determine the center of the rehearsal space that will correspond with the center of the stage. (The director might have to be involved with this as the rehearsal space might not be as big as the stage).

2) Use a dot of spike tape and mark where the center point A is on the floor.

3) Pull one tape out to it's full length, use the locking mechanism on the tape to keep the tape extended, and set it on the floor of the rehearsal space where the front edge of the stage will be (The zero mark on the tape should be at point A).

4) Extend a second tape and put it on the floor on the other side of point A extending to the opposite wall. (You now have two tapes representing the front edge of the stage, that meet at center point A and extend out to the outside walls.)

5) Open and lock a third tape, place it on the floor in the position of the center line with the zero mark at center point A. (Now, you have the line at the front of the stage and the center line on both the floor plan and the rehearsal space floor.)

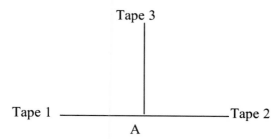

Tape 3

Tape 1 ————————————— Tape 2

A

Using a ½ inch scale, lets try to figure where to put the couch on the following floor plan.

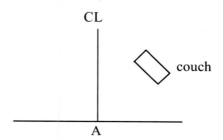

CL

couch

A

STEPS TO TAPING THE FLOOR

1) First you need to take a right angle triangle (which has a 90° angle), place it on the floor plan with one side of the 90° angle running along the center line and the second side of the angle extending out toward the couch.

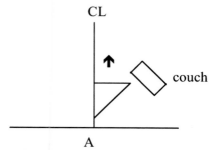

CL

couch

A

2) Slide the triangle up the center line until the second side reaches the corner of the couch.

3) Using a pencil, make a line from the corner of the couch to the center line (line B-C on the next diagram).

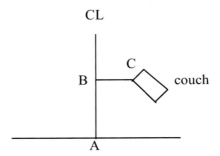

4) Use your ruler and measure up the center line from A to point B. (Let us say that it is 4 inches from A to B, which would mean 8 feet in a ½" scale.)
5) Measure from B to C. (Let us say that it is 2 and ½ inches, which would be 5 feet.)

> SM TIP: As you are making the measurements on the floor plan, note them next to the corresponding letter. Then when you move into the theatre (or a different rehearsal space) you will have all the measurements on your floor plan, and will just have to tape out the floor.

6) Go to the actual rehearsal space floor, measure from the center point up the CL tape 8 feet.
7) Using a fourth tape measure you put the zero mark on the CL tape at 8 feet and extend it stage left on the floor, so that it is horizontal to the front line (BC on our example).
8) Measure along the forth tape 5 feet, and put a small piece of spike tape at the 5' mark on the rehearsal space floor. (You now have Point C, the first corner of your couch.)
9) Repeat steps 1-8 for DE.

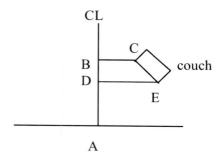

10) Continue through the floor plan point by point.

You now have the two front corners of the couch spiked and can set the couch on those points.

Use this same technique for a wall. Measure the two ends of a wall (or corners). Put the two pieces of tape on the floor to mark the two ends, then, connect the two small pieces of tape with a long piece of tape. You now have a taped line on your rehearsal floor that corresponds to the wall on your floor plan. You continue with these same steps over and over as you work your way through the set pieces and setting.

If you have a door, measure and mark both sides of it. Leave the space for the "actual" door empty (no tape.) Then, take a piece of tape that is the same length as the actual door, and put it at an angle from the side of the door where the hinges are (the actors will now know which way the door opens). You can put an arrow on the floor.

wall   door opening   wall

SM TIP: It is a long process to tape a complicated floor plan. Sometimes you need to allow several hours to do it. Do not wait until the day of the first rehearsal.

CHAPTER FIVE

☑RUNNING REHEARSALS

Your job during rehearsals is to make sure that everything goes smoothly. A smooth-running rehearsal will make all the participants from the director to the actors feel that the stage manager is enabling them to do their jobs to the best of their abilities. You must always have a calm demeanor. Everything may be going crazy around you, but you must remain calm.

> SM TIP: As stated previously, at the beginning of each rehearsal, you need to check the sign in sheet. Sometimes, you have to remind people. You want to get them to the point where they sign in automatically. It is important for later in the process (during performances) that the cast understands that they must always sign in. Otherwise, you may be hunting for actors when you should be preparing to call a show.

GETTING REHEARSALS STARTED

The rehearsal begins at the specified start time. In other words, actors should not be just arriving at this time, but be settled and ready to go. Make sure you get the actors ready for the first rehearsal scene at the appropriate time. Always set up for the first scene prior to the rehearsal so you are ready to go as well. If (for whatever reason) you don't know what the director will be doing first, set up general set pieces that are used for all scenes. Then, the moment the director arrives, ask them what exact scene you will be doing and set it up quickly.

> SM TIP: Do not wait for the director to tell you to get the rehearsal started. Right before you call the actors to the "set", check to see if the director is ready to begin. They may need a moment to collect their thoughts or finish a note.

LATENESS

During rehearsals and performances, you will have to deal with people showing up late for a call. This could be actors, crew - or even the director.

If the time for rehearsal has arrived and an actor is not present, you should wait five minutes and then call them. If they do not answer the phone, assume they are on the way. If you should happen to wake an actor with your call, express to them to come *immediately*. Once they arrive, get the actor into the rehearsal as soon as possible. During a break, point out to this actor that they are not only missing rehearsal time, but taking rehearsal time away from the director and the other actors. Explain in no uncertain terms that you expect this to be the last time it happens.

You should ask the director what they would like you to do in the event that *they* are late for a rehearsal. This time could be used to work on lines, such as by doing a "line through" of the scenes the director is going to rehearse.

Once the show is into technical rehearsals and performances, you may have to deal with tardy crew members. Approach them the same way you did any late actors.

REHEARSAL PROTOCOL

The stage manager "runs" the rehearsal from when to take a break to giving an actor a "line". Each of these aspects seem to be minor, but if they are done incorrectly, can cause major problems in rehearsals.

CALLING CUES DURING REHEARSALS

It will help you enormously, once the actual technical aspects of the show are included, if you have prepared the cast during rehearsals.

Lights

You should always say "lights up" and "lights out" at the beginning and end of each scene. At the very beginning of the play, i.e. "top of the show", go through the motions of calling the cues. Say, "House to half; house out; stage lights to black; actors enter in blackout; lights up". In this way, the actors get use to the idea of entering the stage in the dark. Once you get to techs you will remind them of this procedure, but they will already have heard you say it so often, they should be ready for it.

Sound

Often, a show will have important sound cues, not just ambient sound. You may receive a CD from your sound designer. If you do, all the cues should be on separate tracks so you can "cue them up" *prior* to a rehearsal and not *during* a rehearsal. Other times, you will be making sounds vocally to indicate a sound cue. Anything from bagpipes to toilets flushing could be part of the show.

Music

It may be you are doing a musical with prerecorded music. Again, it is necessary to have the cues on a CD, in order to be able to play them as needed. If you are using a rehearsal pianist, you might have the music recorded for when they cannot attend. In those instances, you will be running the music on a CD player or even a laptop.

BREAKS

If you are working on an Actor's Equity Association (Equity) show, there are specific rules governing when and how long for breaks. In any other situation, it is best to discuss it with the director prior to the first rehearsal.

Many theatres follow the Equity rule of a five-minute break after every fifty-five minutes of rehearsal or a ten-minute break after every eighty minutes of rehearsal. Some directors like to be warned before you call a break. Some will want you to use your discretion and, for example, call a break after they finish one scene, even if it has only been seventy minutes, so you do not have to stop the next scene rehearsal after only ten minutes.

As a stage manager, you sometimes do not get a break; there is usually a problem that needs to be dealt with during that time. Often, it is setting up for the next scene. If you have an assistant, what you can do is have them set up the next scene, while you take a break, then let them take one after you and the actors come back.

SM TIP: ANTICIPATION. A stage manager that can anticipate the next scene, or where the director is going next, is worth their weight in gold. Pay careful attention to how the director likes to work during rehearsals. Patterns will develop that you can then use as "cues" during subsequent rehearsals. If you are working through the entire play in chronological order, you know what scene is next. If you know the director's "cue" for when they are finishing the current scene, then, all you have to do is quickly verify with the director that they are "moving on", and you are ready to change the set or props.

GIVING LINES

As the actors start to memorize their lines, they will need to call for them when they are stuck trying to remember their next line. It is important that you explain to the actors that they need to say "line" in order for you to know to give them their line. "What is it?" is not an appropriate way to call for line. If you find the actors doing this, remind them nicely that you would like them to just say "line". You should also not *assume* when to give lines. If, for example, there is a silence or a pause in the ongoing dialogue or scene, the actor may be just "acting" (in the moment). If, in that instance, you say the appropriate next line you may get a stern reproach from the actor or director. A good "rule of thumb" is to not give a line during a silence until the director *says* to give it.

When you are giving an actor a line, do not give them a "line reading". Say it loud and clear, and without inflection.

Whenever a scene is being run, your concentration should be focused on giving lines. If you take your eyes off the script for a second, chances are *that* is when an actor calls for a line. If you have an assistant, you can give them this job - just make sure they know how to do it.

RUN THROUGHS

Several times during the rehearsal process there will be a *run through* of the entire show, meaning starting at the beginning of the play ("House to half") and running, without stopping for mistakes, through to the end ("Lights out"). Arrive at least forty-five minutes prior to the beginning time. Sweep the stage and set up all the props on tables, ready for a run. During the run, any set changes should be coordinated ahead of time with the stage management staff so that all changes go quickly and smoothly. At the end of Act I, set up Act II, before you give your staff a break.

RUNNING ORDER

When preparing for a run through, make a list of the scenes (and musical numbers within each) to post backstage for the cast. This will help them keep the sequence of scenes correct in their minds. You can enlarge them, so they are easy to read.

LINE NOTES

At some point in the rehearsal process, the director will ask you to note lines that are being said incorrectly. Usually, it will be during a run through. You can do this as you give lines by having a pencil in your hand and noting in the margins the places where the actor: calls for line, inverts words or lines, or skips words or lines. You can develop your own shorthand so after the run, you can either 1) type up the line notes for the actors, or 2) give them orally to the actors at a time designated by the director.

LINE THROUGHS

Once the cast is off book (i.e. has the show memorized), the director may ask you to hold *line throughs*: the process of going through the script line by line without blocking. You or your assistant can do this. It is very important that you make sure the actors are saying the correct lines, so they don't get into the habit of paraphrasing. If an actor has habitually said the wrong word in a line, this is an excellent opportunity for you to give them the correct word. Directors will want you to stop the line through if an actor messes up a line. Then, you give the correct line and have the actors start with the line *before* the one that is being corrected. Don't start with the line *after* the corrected one or the actor will do the same mistake the next rehearsal. You want to make sure the actor "says" the corrected line.

REHEARSAL REPORT

The designers and staff are not at every rehearsal. Therefore, it is important that you take notes for the director, and then make sure everybody receives the notes. To facilitate this process, most stage managers will use an email, containing the director's notes, that goes out to all of the design and technical staff, as well as the director, assistant stage managers, and producer. It is important to have sections for every major technical aspect of the show, music, dance, combat, and any other area that may be relevant.

Make sure that you check with the director before you send out the rehearsal report. This can be done during the rehearsal. They may say to you, "Make a note about the light for the lighting designer." Confirm right then if it should be included in the notes. It may be the director wants to talk in person to the designer and wants you to remind them to do just that.

The following is a sample of a typical rehearsal report.

SOME SWEET DAY
RAMAPO COLLEGE OF NEW JERSEY

REHEARSAL REPORT #8   Tuesday, 4/13/07

Start time: 6:00 pm   End time: 10:30 pm
    Breaks: 6:55-7:00, 8:15-8:25, 9:15-9:20
ATTENDANCE:
    CREW--Director, Asst. Director, SM, ASM
    CAST--Full Cast (Joe-:15 late-traffic)
Absences: None
WORK ACCOMPLISHED:
    Act I, Scene 1:   Work Blocking, 130 minutes
    Act I, Scene 5:   Initial Blocking, 50 minutes
    Act I, Scene 7:   Initial Blocking, 70 minutes

PRODUCTION NOTES
GENERAL: Production Meeting on Monday, 4/19
                in Sharp Theatre at 1 pm
LIGHTS: No notes
SET: Do we have escape stairs off the mound?
SOUND: Will we have body mics?
COSTUMES: Do we need to schedule "fittings" for
                White Knight costumes?
PROPS: Can we get the hoes taped?—splinters
MUSIC: Recordings of the accompaniment?
RUN THROUGH for Designers: Friday, 4/16, 8:00
NEXT REHEARSAL: Wednesday, April 14, 6-11

SM TIP: Do not assume that everyone diligently reads the rehearsal report. Send a follow up email, or drop by the shop (where the technical work is being done) to touch bases. Nothing should drop through the cracks as relates to notes from the director. If you follow through, the director will soon realize that you are making sure the production does not hit any snags.

SCENE WORK LOG

It helps to keep a running list of work accomplished on scenes (or songs if doing a musical). You list all of the scenes on the left hand side of a scene work log and leave the rest of it blank. Then, when you work on a scene you write in the date and what was accomplished. This gives you (and the director) a visual idea of the work that has been done and which scenes have been worked more than others. You can label the top row in whatever way works with your production: some directors will do table work before blocking a scene, others like to jump right in with blocking.

SCENE WORK LOG *SHOW TITLE*					
ACT I	Table Work	Blocked	Work	Work	Run
Scene 1	4/10/08	4/12/08	4/17/08		
Scene 2	4/10/08	4/12/08	4/17/08		
Scene 3	4/11/08	4/13/08			
Scene 4	4/11/08	4/13/08			
Scene 5	4/10/08	4/12/08	4/17/08		
Scene 6	4/10/08	4/12/08	4/17/08		
Scene 7	4/10/08	4/12/08	4/17/08		
Scene 8	4/11/08	4/13/08			

CHAPTER SIX

☑BLOCKING NOTATION

Neatness counts.

Nothing is ever written in ink in a prompt script.

These are the rules to live by when taking blocking notation. When the director starts blocking the show, they may talk in specific or general terms. Either way, you must notate in your prompt script every move that they give to the actors. It will most likely change several times before the show opens, but it has to be written down from the first step.

In this chapter I will give you ideas for easy ways to take down blocking notation. But before you start writing you need to make sure your script is ready.

PROMPT BOOK, TOO

At this point in the process you should have your prompt script ready to go. It should be in your prompt book: a three-ring binder with labeled tabs to make it easy for you to find any needed items. In addition, you should put tabs into the script itself to mark every scene and act. You can thumb through the script and efficiently turn to any scene the director wishes to work on at that moment.

Put tabs on blank pieces of paper so you can tab paperwork that changes regularly (e.g. daily rehearsal schedules). Any paperwork generated should find its spot in the prompt book.

The following is a list of items needed in your prompt book by the time the show opens.

Contact Sheet
Cast List
Rehearsal Schedule
Production Schedule
Script with Blocking Notation
Rehearsal Notes
List of Musical Numbers
Prop List
Costume Changes
Lighting Notes (e.g. "Cheat Sheet")
Running Lists for tech changes

Plus any papers that have been distributed to the cast/crew during the process.

HOW TO TAKE BLOCKING NOTATION

When the director is blocking, it is imperative that you give them your undivided attention. You cannot be working on a rehearsal schedule, or a prop list while doing this. It is very similar to taking notes in a lecture class where you must listen to every word the lecturer says, and note almost all of them.

One of the most important aspects of taking blocking notation is to have a pencil and a great eraser. (An artist eraser is recommended because it will not eat up your paper.) It is the director's prerogative to change the blocking. Most directors will do this every once in a while. Some directors will do it all the time. Therefore, it is important that you are very exact in how you notate the blocking.

The blocking should be written on the right hand side of the script—unless you are left handed, and then you might want to reverse your script and have the text on the left hand side of the binder. The blocking should always be written *outside* the text so it is easy to find. You should print anything you write in your script as neatly as you possibly can. (Taking a set design course will help you to learn neat penmanship in a theatrical context because of the printing requirements inherent in the course.)

> SM TIP: You should always make sure that you are paying attention to the director and the rehearsal. Let actors know that during a rehearsal is not the time to approach you with a problem (e.g. needing to check blocking notation). It is very distracting to the director to have people talking (even if it is quietly).

THEATRICAL SHORTHAND

It will help if you develop shorthand that is universal to all theatre persons.

SR means stage right
SL means stage left
CS means center stage
DS means down stage
US means up stage
USC means up stage center
X means to cross (move from one point to another)

Beyond the above, you should figure out shorthand for your show's characters' names. For example, Richard III could be RIII. Or Harry might just be H. Then, Henry would be HE or HY. By using a key at the beginning of your script, and always noting who is doing the move (e.g. H X DR, meaning "Harry crosses down right"), you will save a lot of time during rehearsal by not having to write out every word.

The other shorthand note that I suggest is putting a circle around any characters' shorthand initial. This will accomplish two things: it will allow you to find the character quickly on the page and it will prevent confusion between a character initial (e.g. a D for 'David') and a stage direction.

PLACEMENT OF BLOCKING NOTATION

Let's say the director specifies blocking for particular parts of a line of dialogue, e.g. "at the *beginning* of this line..." Make a hash mark (/) at the beginning of that line and underline the line of dialogue during which the cross takes place.

HARRY
/How do you know I took the paper? X DSR

If the director says, "at the *end* of this line…" then you would place the (/) hash mark after the last word of that line and draw a line to the movement associated with that moment.

HARRY
How do you know I took the paper?/ X DSR

If the director says, "somewhere around here…" then don't make a hash mark, and write the blocking down in the margins next to the line or paragraph they mention. If there is a question at a later rehearsal, you can say with confidence where the director originally asked for the move to happen.

CHANGES IN BLOCKING

When the blocking is altered during another rehearsal, it is imperative that you make note of the new line of dialogue where the movement begins. You can erase the original place-ment OR you can strike through it with a light pencil mark. (If the director wants to come back to the original position, you will have it in your script.) Then when the scene has been worked several times and the blocking is no longer changing, you can choose to erase the original and any other versions.

Sometimes the director will ask you to take notes of any missed blocking during a run through. In this situation, ask the director if they want you to give them the list after the run through or to give it directly to the actors.

During a "working" rehearsal (as opposed to a run), after a scene has been blocked, the director might ask you to tell them if the actor has missed a move, or changed where during the scene the move is made. In this situation, you can quietly notify the director when an actor makes a mistake and the director can then choose what to do next. The director might ignore the mis-take, for example, or they might even tell you to change it in the blocking script because they like it better this way.

USING A FLOOR PLAN

You can ask the technical director or set designer if they can print a one-quarter inch floor plan on letter size paper. Copy it and shrink it down so it takes up only one half of the paper. Put two copies of the small floor plan onto one piece of paper. Your multiple floor plan sheet will look like this:

Floor plan key: ▭ bench   ◯ tree   ☐ podium
                   ⟶ ▶ ——— church with door

Put this opposite every page of the script, with the script to the right, and the floor plan sheet to the left. Then, when the director is blocking, you can make a little diagram on each floor plan as to where everyone is at that moment of the play. The "two floor plan sheet" is useful because the director usually has multiple stage moves for every page. It is most helpful in large-scale shows and musicals. If you have twenty people on stage, you don't have to make a list of where each actor is at every moment. You can also make one with three floor plans on it.

SM TIP: The important thing to know about blocking is to always write down what the director says to the actors. Sometimes you have to get up out of your chair and follow the director up on the stage in order to accomplish this.

PART THREE

TECHNICAL ASPECTS

CHAPTER SEVEN

☑ORGANIZING THE TECH

The actual organizing of the technical aspects began the moment you started your tech lists at the beginning of your pre-production work. Those lists will be in your prompt book and help you to develop the running lists needed for performances. As rehearsals progress toward the technical rehearsals, you should be adding to your lists and determining the exact placement for sounds, props, set pieces, costume pieces and light changes. You should keep lists in chronological order and separate *until* you are going into your technical rehearsals.

Make sure to keep in touch with the designers and department heads during the build phase of the production. Don't assume that putting something on the rehearsal report will insure that the person responsible understands the note. Stay in contact with all the heads of the departments. Checking in on a regular basis is highly recommended.

PROPS

During rehearsals you should have your original prop list in your prompt book. You will add to this list as the director adds props to the show. It is very seldom that a director will *not* add a prop at some point during the rehearsal process. Make sure to note this in your rehearsal report and then add it to your prop list.

KEEPING TRACK OF PROP CHANGES

Keeping track of the prop changes/movements is one of the hardest jobs you will have to do during rehearsals. If you have an assistant, have them concentrate on props during rehearsals. But this is not a way for you to ignore this aspect.

SM TIP: The prop person is in charge of finding or building of props. The running of them falls under the jurisdiction of the stage manager. You can use an assistant to keep the rehearsal space and backstage organized, but do not expect them to be in overall control of the props, they are your responsibility.

As rehearsals continue you should note which props start where, who moves them, and where they end up. Anytime a prop is handled by an actor, it should be noted if it is moved in any way.

To help keep track of the changing props during the play, take a post it, label it "props", and put one opposite the first page of each scene. Then, you list on it where all the props are at the beginning of that scene. Do this, because you do not always work the play chronologically. If the director shows up to rehearsal and says, "I want to start with scene three today", you do not have to look through your script for all the prop movements leading up to scene three. You have the opening placement on your post it, and can set it up quickly and efficiently.

DIGITAL PICTURES

If you have a digital camera and computer, take a picture during a break of a rehearsal of the setting for the beginnings of each scene, print the pictures and put them in your binder opposite the first page of each scene. You should do this for the beginnings of every scene in the same way you would list all the props on a post it. Do not do this too early in the process, as the props will change as blocking is changing. If you get to the point where there is continuity to the scenes, without changes being made every rehearsal, then that would be a good time to take pictures. Some directors will be making changes until the very last minute, and this will not be a viable option.

PRELIMINARY PROP RUNNING LIST

As rehearsals progress, you need to start a preliminary prop running list, which will include every prop, its placement at the top of the show, any movement it makes, the ending position, and comments. This list should be filled in as the positions or movements change. The comment section is for special notes. For example, an actor does not have time to return a prop to the prop table. You would make a note that an assistant stage manager needs to "catch" the appropriate prop as the actor exits the stage. This list could end up being many pages long. It is very important that you keep it updated throughout rehearsals.

As the production is getting closer to technical rehearsals, you need to finalize your prop running list. At this point, you will no longer list each prop in the order they are used, but by the placement on the stage and backstage, preshow, during the scenes, at intermission, and at the end of the show. This information is all included on your preliminary prop running list that you have been formulating throughout rehearsals.

PROP RUNNING LIST

This list will be a sequential listing of all the prop moves and notes to help the show run smoothly. It should have everything that is needed to have every prop in the correct place from curtain up to curtain down.

This list will start you off for technical rehearsals. You will make copies and give to your ASM and any running crew that will be working backstage. Once technical rehearsals start, you may need to update the lists. Sometimes the placement of props change during the course of organizing the technical aspects.

As you write your running list, you need to note when the moves actually happen. If it is at the end of a scene or during a scene.

After technical rehearsals, you should always get the

crew together to see if any changes need to be made. As usual, always date your lists. That way when you revise it everyone will know which list is the most recent. A partial Prop Running List follows:

PRELIMINARY PROP RUNNING LIST   Date
SOME SWEET DAY   Page ___ of ___

Act/ Scene	Prop	Place	Move	Ending Position	Comments
I/1	4 Hoes	USR Table	Actors	USL Table	
	6 Hoes	SR Table	Actors	SR Table	
	2 Hoes	USL Table	Actors	SR Table	
	6 Hoes	SL Table	Actors	SL Table	ASM "catch" Isaac's DSR
	Bucket	Preset DSR		SR Table	Set at edge of stage—Actor strikes
	Gun	SR Table	Buddy	USR Table	ASM catch shotgun & hand jug to Buddy USR
I/2	Jug	USR Table	Buddy	SL Table	Actor strikes
I/3	Poem	USR Table	Max	USR Table	

PROP TABLES

As your rehearsals progress you may see the need to put up prop tables in the rehearsal hall. These tables should be set stage right and left. You will place on each of them the props that come from the corresponding side of the stage. On the table itself, in order to start getting ready for running the show, you can place masking tape around each prop and label said prop. In this way, if an actor or crew person has to pick up and/or return a prop, they will know the exact place for it to live. It is also easier to see what props are missing if everything has a labeled place on the tables.

> SM TIP: While working through these lists you may discover moves that happen backstage. For instance, a prop may get struck from scene 3 off stage right and placed by the actor on the SR prop table. Then, two scenes later it needs to come on from SL with another actor. Note on the running list that the prop needs to move from the SR prop table to the SL prop table during the scene.

SET PIECES AND SET CHANGES

As with the prop list, you will also have a list of set changes/set pieces. How complicated the set changes and set pieces are will depend on the set design. Get a copy of the design plans from the technical director or the set designer. This could include: floor plan, renderings, detail drawings. You really only need the floor plan, but renderings are also helpful. Update your preliminary set/set pieces list to include all the information that the designer has included in their work.

You will then start to organize your set change sheet. This list will include: who does what, when, in what order, from where, and to where. The more this can be finalized prior to tech rehearsals the better. Don't rely on a technical director or designer to do this, although in some community theatres the technical director will be responsible for set change assignments. Sometimes, the director will do part of it, in the situation where actors are required to move pieces of furniture.

Be aware that the director may also make some changes to the set design, by *moving* chairs, tables, etc. from one part of the stage to the next. Make sure that this information is relayed to the set designer by the director or yourself.

The director may *add* chairs or stools, etc. during a

rehearsal. Again, you need to communicate this information to the designer.

For this section, I would like to approach it using different scenarios depending on the style of production. Scenario One is for a unit set with few changes. Scenario Two is for a unit set with many changes of set pieces. Scenario Three is for a multiple set show with many changes. Some shows have no changing sets but furniture only. In that situation, you should look at Scenario Two for multiple changes.

SCENARIO ONE:

You have a unit set with no major changes of the set itself. In this case you will make a list of all the set pieces (furniture, etc.) and notate their placement at the top of the show. If they are changed by the actors during the run of the show, you need to note that on post its at the beginning of each scene. Like with your props post its, you want to note where everything is at the top of a scene in case the director wants to work on a scene out of sequence. If they are changed by the crew at scene breaks or intermission, then you need to note them on your set change lists.

This list, like the prop running list, is a comprehensive listing of all the set pieces, when and where they move during a production. It is a very simple scenario, and you might actually chose to combine this with your prop running list.

SCENARIO TWO:

You have a unit set with set pieces changing throughout the play by the actors or crew. In this case, your list of set pieces will be notated for each scene. Who moves them should also be noted. For instance if an actor moves a chair for the next scene, you would note it.

Sometimes, a director will incorporate the actors into the set changes. In that way, you may not need as many crew members. They has decided to make it a directorial decision that they will choreograph for the production. You will note what the director assigns to which actor, and then, write it in the set change list. Make sure you keep your list of set pieces with you, sometimes a director will miss a piece of furniture. You need to double check each move that they direct to make sure nothing has been missed.

> SM TIP: If the director does choose to use the actors, it would be best to make any assignments early in the process. In that way, the actors will be rehearsing the set changes along with the acting. Yet again, it will make the technical rehearsals run smoother.

In this scenario, I would suggest that you have a separate set change list for each transition. In this way, everyone involved from cast to crew will know what they are doing for the set changes and when.

SCENARIO THREE:

You have a multiple set show where things fly in and out, roll on and off, or a complete change is made between acts. This is a very intricate scenario, but as with any of the complicated aspects of this job, if you make sure to keep ahead of everything with lists and organization it can go very smoothly when you get to technical rehearsals.

This type of production may have many crew members as well as cast members making moves during set changes. Once again, you need to find out from the director and technical director, who will be doing the changes. If you can figure out all of the changes *before* you get to the technical rehearsals, then they will go a lot smoother.

You need to make sure to clearly note what is struck at each change, what is moved and what is set for the first time. If you look at it as a moving puzzle, you can have one crew person do more that one move. For instance, they might carry on a chair that is being added to the set, and then strike a table off stage that is no longer used. When you have a large crew and everyone is only doing one thing the change will be accomplished quickly. Whereas, if you are trying to keep the number of crew members to a minimum, you might have each crew member do multiple tasks during each change.

The main thing to remember about working out the set changes, no matter which scenario you have, is to make sure everything is covered. Rehearse it during rehearsals with actors so they are not doing something brand new when they get into technical rehearsals. Type everything ahead of time. It's OK to make changes, but if will help you to organize all the technical aspects before you get into the techs.

SPIKING THE SET PIECES

Once a decision is made by the director and/or set designer as to the actual placement of set pieces (e.g. tables and chairs) it is important that you spike the rehearsal space and/or stage with spike tape to mark their positions.

You can use a 1" piece of tape for the two back legs of chairs. No need to do every leg. The same with couches and coffee tables. A dining room or kitchen table that has a pedestal bottom to it, instead of legs, you can put a 2" X for its position.

If there are numerous set pieces that move throughout the show, you may need to color code the different scenes, blue for Act One, red for Act Two. If you need to, you can use a permanent marker to write what piece of furniture or which scene on each piece of tape.

As rehearsals progress, the director may deem it necessary to move set pieces to different positions. Make sure to take up the old tape and put down new. When you move to the stage during tech rehearsals you need to make sure to spike the furniture again.

SCENE CHANGE SHEETS

For any of the previous scenarrios, you should put together a set change sheet (a.k.a. scene shift sheet). These sheets can be used by the stage management team to organize changes during run throughs. If the director is using actors to move scenery, then the scene change sheets will assist them in understanding the moves in a visual format. Eventually, you will make copies for anyone who is helping with the scene changes during the production.

Similar to the multiple floor plan, these sheets have the

floor plan in a smaller scale. The difference is you now show how the pieces of the set change from one scene to the next. The following is the set change sheet for *Some Sweet Day*, Scene 6 to Scene 7.

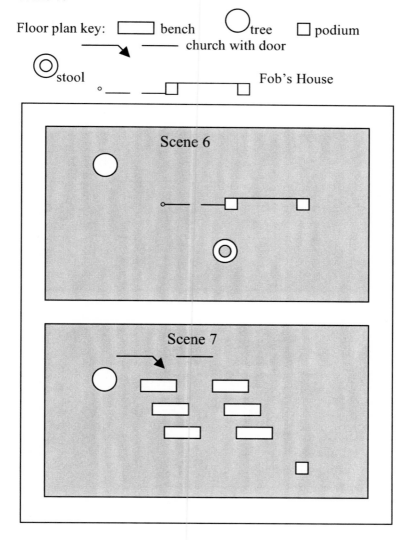

> SM TIP: Once the director has made assignments for the moving of the set pieces, you can put the actor's names on the sheet and give them a copy. Then, post copies backstage, so when there is a run through they will have a place to check their assignments without having to carry the papers.

The following is the transition from Scene 6 to Scene 7.

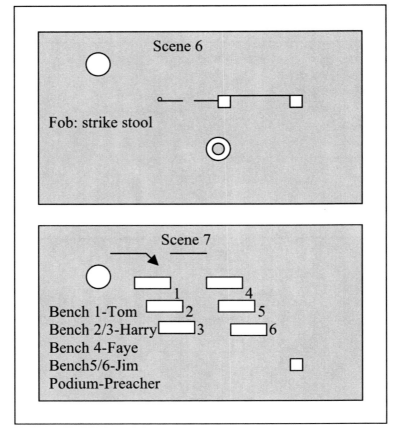

Sometime, there is only one scene shown per page. This is up to your discretion.

COSTUMES

You may not see them very often, but a good working relationship with the costume designer can cultivate a very healthy technical rehearsal. Throughout the rehearsal process you will be organizing the actors and any fittings or other costume needs that they have. You should contact the costume designer prior to the beginning of rehearsals and find out how they would like to proceed from measurements to final fittings.

When you are scheduling actors for costume fittings or measurements, you need to make sure that all parties concerned know the time they are needed. The actors need to know that they should not be late because the designer will be seeing several actors in a row. One person late will make everyone late. The designer needs to know which actor is coming at what time, so that they are prepared for that character.

SM TIP: I cannot overemphasize how important this thread of communication is to the show. Costume designers spend lots of time out and around shopping from store to store. The time they have to complete the costumes is usually limited. They do not need to be wasting time, waiting for actors. So remind the actors at the end of rehearsals of any costume fittings, send them an email, and maybe you might send a text message as well.

MEASUREMENTS

The costume designer will need to meet with each actor individually in order to get accurate measurements and sizes for their costumes. This process usually takes 15-20 minutes per actor. Sometimes the designer will ask that time be set aside during the first rehearsal to accomplish this task. You need to check with the director in this situation. Many directors don't want to lose time during the first rehearsal while actors go off one at a time to have measurements taken. If, that is the case, you need to organize with the designer a time convenient for the actors to come to the costume shop for measurements.

FITTINGS

Throughout the rehearsal process, the costume designer will need to see each actor to try on their costumes. Sometimes an actor will have one fitting, and other times they will need three or four. All of them should be scheduled through the stage manager.

You do not have to be in attendance at the fittings. But, you must follow through with the designer to make sure that the actors are showing up and are punctual. If they are not, you need to talk to the actors.

COSTUME PIECES

If your actors are going to be working in skirts or with capes or coats, etc., it is important to organize rehearsal costume pieces for them to use. If it is a long skirt, you can ask the actor if she can bring one in from home and leave it for rehearsals. If it is high heels, you may want to do the same thing. If an actor has to work with a cape, you should contact the costume designer and see if the theatre has some costume "stock" from which you could pull a cape or two for rehearsals. As with props, it is very important that you make sure that every costume piece that is held (e.g. purses), that is taken off (e.g. winter coat), or put on (e.g. hat) and will affect the actors movement and timing, needs to be available from the beginning of rehearsals. You will not get the actual costume until technical rehearsals. So you might have to do with an old bed sheet (like when you played Superman/woman in the second grade.)

COSTUME CHANGES

Most likely the costume designer will have costume change sheets for each of the actors. If so, they should give you a copy. These sheets will have everything that an actor wears for each scene. By looking at these you can determine during which scenes or scene changes the actor will have their costume changes. If there are changes other than ones that will take place at intermission in the dressing rooms, you need to make a list/note of any quick changes that must occur. By looking through your script, you should be able to determine how much time an actor will have for their change. If there is time for them to go back to their dressing room, they can probably do the change without assistance. If you note that an actor has only a few lines of dialogue in which to make their change, you need to make that known to the costume designer. Most likely, the designer already knows this. But, never assume. Communication with the designer will ultimately save precious time during technical rehearsals. Once you and the designer have noted which changes are occuring where, you need to determine if a wardrobe person is needed backstage for costume changes. Sometimes, you will need more than one person because of the number of simultaneous changes. You might need to ask other actors to help as well.

SM EXPERIENCE: I did a show that was 90 minutes long with no intermission. It had five actors playing 35 characters and 49 costume changes. We had costume changes in the wings every few pages of text. I wrote up all the changes as either "lots of time" (more than 1 minute), "little time" (1 minute), or "quick" (less than 1 minute). The costume designer was ecstatic that I took the time to do this. It helped immensely during the tech and dress rehearsals.

QUICK CHANGES

For those times when the actor has only a few seconds in which to make the change you will need to discuss with the tech director the appropriate place backstage for a changing booth. This changing booth should have curtains around it and a carpeted floor. You will also possibly need a chair and hooks or a rack on which to hang costumes. A mirror is needed to check hair, etc.. Make sure the area you choose has adequate lighting (backstage blues).

You will need to organize the changing booth backstage, as well as, which crew member helps which actor, etc. for every change made with the assistance of a crew person.

LIGHTS

You will probably have very little as far as lists are concerned for lights. During the rehearsals you have been saying "Lights Up", and "Blackout" and such. Until you get into the technical rehearsal, the lighting will not be much of an issue.

SPECIALS

Often, a director will want a special light on a character at a certain moment in the play. You will need to note that in your rehearsal report. Then, at some point, you will need to put a piece of tape on the floor in the spot where the special is needed, so that the lighting designer can focus the light for that spot. You can offer to come to the stage and meet with the lighting designer to show them the exact placement.

SOUND

As noted in chapter five, if there are audio cues that happen within the script (e.g. car horns) you will have been making the sounds throughout the rehearsal process. It is possible that the director and/or sound designer have chosen specific songs to play during the scenes. If this is the case, it is important to try and get copies during the rehearsal process. If the actors need to become accustomed to certain music and music cues, then by using the music during the acting rehearsals the technical rehearsals will go smoother.

REHEARSAL SOUND

Sometimes, you will actually have CDs to play during the rehearsal process and other times, you will not hear the music or sound (e.g. crickets) until the technical rehearsals. If you are required to play sound/music during rehearsals, you need to have one of the following: a CD player, a laptop computer with CD, or an IPOD with speakers. It should be set up prior to the start of each rehearsal. You also need to make sure you practice and have the CDs organized and/or cued to the correct track prior to the beginning of the rehearsal. There is nothing worse than the director and actors expecting sounds and they are two or three seconds late. It is important for the flow and rhythm of the rehearsal that any sound or music cue happens when it is *supposed* to happen.

You will probably not have the sound cues for set changes until tech, but you should be aware of them.

SOUND CUE LIST

The designer may give you a list of the sound cues being used for the production. If that is the case and you can get a copy of the cues from the technical director or sound designer, you should take the opportunity to become familiar with all the music and sound. When you get to the tech rehearsals there will possibly be times where there are light cues that are coordinated with the sound at a specific moment in the music. If you have spent time familiarizing yourself with the music, it will be easier for you.

> SM EXPERIENCE: Several times during my career, I have been called on to run the sound board for an absent board op. At other times it was assigned to me from the start.

PHONE RINGS

Often in a show, there will be need of a phone ringing. Sometimes, this is a sound cue. Other times, you are running it using a contact switch in the booth. It is usually a visual cue that you take and is coordinated with the director/actor as to when it will end (e.g. after the second ring the actor picks up the phone).

CUE SCRIPT

You need to prepare a "clean" script to use for technical rehearsals and performances. Do not use the prompt script, as you don't need to have all those notations in your way, when trying to call the show. If you are doing a play, which has no internal cues (just lights up at the beginning of each act and lights down at the end), you can use your blocking script. But, if you are doing a show that will have multiple cues for lights and sound, you should make sure to have a clean copy of the script.

This copy needs to be exactly like your final blocking script. Any line changes should be made in it. You will need to continue to have your prompt book nearby, but once you get to technical rehearsals, your main work will be done in the cue script. It is helpful to have a blank piece of paper at the front of your script on which to write the opening sequence of cues.

CUE LIGHTS

If there is an actor who has to make a blind entrance, meaning it is not on a cue line and they cannot see the stage from their entrance point (e.g. behind a door), then you need to figure out in rehearsals how that actor will be cued. If they can see your ASM, then it could be a visual cue on a hand signal from the ASM. If they cannot see the ASM, you might have to ask the technical director for cue lights. These are very low wattage colored lights that are placed in an appropriate place backstage, so the actor can see them from their entrance position. The stage manager usually runs it from the booth. If it is possible, two lights should go on together. That way if one bulb burns out the other will still work.

It is possible that you will need to cue multiple set moves either from the wings or from the fly rail. Each of them should have their own set of cue lights. If you have multiple cue lights backstage because several things are happening at the same time, they should be different colors so each actor/crew person is following a different light.

The stage manager most often controls cue lights. You will have a row of toggle switches next to the stage managers position in the booth. You will have to coordinate the cue lights with the calling of the light and sound cues. This will be covered in the next chapter.

FINAL RUNNING LIST

By the end of your rehearsal period, you should have a comprehensive running list for every aspect of tech during the performance. Make individual list for the respective crew members. Then, combine all the changes that occur during the show into one master running list. It will have costume changes, set movements, prop moves, and any other technical needs for which a crew person or cast member is responsible. Meet with the technical director to make crew assignments (which crew member will be responsible for each aspect.) Make copies of this list for everyone involved in any of the changes. Date it, as you will update them with changes that are determined during the technical process.

You want to fill these sheets out and make copies for everyone involved so they can highlight their own moves. It is very likely that after the initial technical rehearsal, you will have to retype them. You will discover that one crew person is better at something else and make changes to match them up.

Every time you update the running list, make new copies for the crew members, the technical director, all stage managers and to post back stage.

FINAL Running List

Some Sweet Day   Revised 4/8/07

Pg. 3 of 7

Duty	Object	Person	Cue
TRANSITION INTO SCENE SIX			
Cue: Fob Exits			
Strike	Stool	Fob	as exit
Fly out	Fob's House	Joe	QL
Fly in	Church	Janice	QL
Cue: Fob Off stage			
Set	SR Benches	Tom/Harry	QL
Set	SL Benches	Jim/Faye	QL
Set	Podium	Preacher	QL
Hand out	Fans	Joy/Jane	QL
TRANSITION INTO SCENE SEVEN			
Cue: "Be careful goin' home."			
Strike	SL Bench	Jim/Faye	
Strike	SR Bench	Tom/Harry	
Fly out	Church	Janice	QL
Fly in	Isaac's house	Joe	QL

CHAPTER EIGHT

☑TECHNICAL REHEARSALS

During these rehearsals you will go through the show carefully working on all the technical aspects (lights, sound, set changes, costume changes) sometimes with the actors and sometimes without. You must never forget that technical rehearsals are the first time that you, the crew, and the designers have had the opportunity to put the technical aspects of the show together.

If you have finished putting together a comprehensive running list, you are on your way to a successful technical rehearsal. Technical rehearsals are always long and tedious. The best way to smooth them out is to be organized and ready for them.

GETTING READY FOR TECHS

You have been getting ready for techs since you first opened the script many weeks ago. The following are things that need to happen, just before the tech rehearsals start. Unless otherwise noted, assume you are not responsible for actually doing them or providing them, but make sure *someone* is taking on that responsibility.

1. THE TECH TABLE: A long table (or two) - with lights to read by - in the middle of the house for the director, yourself, the light designer and the sound designer.

2. HEADSETS: There should be headsets set up at the tech table for all members of the design team, as well as in other areas of the theatre for those crew members who are running

lights and sound, and for those backstage, such as your ASM and fly crew.

3. GLOW TAPE: You need to take a moment before everyone arrives for the tech, to put glow tape at appropriate places on the stage and backstage.

4. CLEAN THE THEATRE/STAGE: The stage and backstage need to be clean and clear for the actors. This should be done by you, your ASM, and any of the backstage running crew.

5. CUE SCRIPT: As I said in Chapter Seven, you need to have this organized before the tech.

6. STAGE MANAGEMENT KIT: Make sure you have plenty of pencils, erasers, and a ruler in your kit (see Appendix One).

7. SNACKS: Make sure you have healthy snacks for yourself. Don't let your blood sugar get too low. You must keep a clear head.

8. BACKSTAGE BLUES: Work lights (blue lights) ashould be in place backstage and turned on.

9. MASKING: Check with the technical director to make sure all masking will be in place.

10. DRESSING ROOMS: Put the actor's names in the dressing rooms to let them know which mirror/station they use. You can consult on this with the costume designer.

11. QUICK CHANGE BOOTH: You need to make sure that the areas chosen for quick changes have been set up.

12. GOD MIC: A microphone that feeds into the backstage, auditorium, dressing rooms, green room and shop. This will help you to keep control over the technical rehearsals.

13. CUE LIGHTS: You may need cue lights backstage in order to cue either actor's entrances or fly moves or even live sounds. Before tech, you need to let the technical director or master electrician know if you anticipate a need for cue lights.

14. SOUND PROOFING: Sometimes it is necessary to put down pieces of carpeting backstage to keep the sound of heels, etc. to a minimum.

GOD MIC

Hopefully, the theatre has a so-called God mic. Throughout the tech process, you will need to make announcements over it. Always speak clearly. Enunciate every word you say. End every transmission with a "Thank you." Good manners on the God mic will go a long way with both cast and crew.

When rehearsing scenes during tech, you will be stopping and starting the action on stage. When you want the tech to stop you say, "Hold". Once you have finished the work needed (e.g. writing the cue), you announce where in the script the actors should pick the action back up; the light and sound board operators need to know what cue to be in; and the backstage running crew needs to know the setting. When the tech people are ready to résumé, you tell the crew to "standby" and then, say to the actors, "Actor's Go".

> SM TIP: This process that you will follow in technical rehearsals should be explained to everyone (cast and crew) prior to the start of tech. The actors should be told to stay in place and not to talk when a "hold" is called. They need to understand that a hold means necessary work is being done (and they musn't treat it as a break from rehearsal). At some point during the tech, you may have to remind the actors to stay in place and not talk. Assume that they are bored standing on the stage and *aren't* doing it just to be a pain.

GLOW TAPE

Prior to the tech, cut a portion of the glow tape into small pieces (¼" and ½" thickness). Go around and put pieces backstage and on stage where you think an actor might not be able to see a set piece corner. By walking around the backstage area and imagining it is dark, you will detect many places where an actor or crew person could trip or bump into something. Inevitably, during the tech, an actor will find the one piece that you missed and bump into it, or trip over it. The ASM should have the glow tape and scissors near them during the techs. The actors should be told to let the ASM know where they had a problem seeing something in the dark. Then, during a pause in the action, the ASM can cut pieces of the tape and put them where needed. (The ASM could keep some cut pieces in their pocket for this situation.)

TYPES OF TECHNICAL REHEARSALS

Every theatre has its own style of organizing technical rehearsals. Some have dry techs, others have dress techs, and some have both. You need to discuss with your technical director how the techs will be done. The following are different types of tech rehearsals.

DRY TECH

The dry tech is a rehearsal for the technical staff and crew, without actors. Sometimes you will go through the show and work through all the set changes, lighting and sound cues. Other times you will spend the time getting ready for a tech with actors the following day.

Before you can actually start running set changes, it is important that the crew members be familiar with the aspect of tech for which they will be responsible. The "follow spot" operators (a.k.a. "ops") should have time to "play" with the follow spot to make sure they know how to run them. If there are several pieces of scenery flying in and out during the show, the fly men and women should be shown how the fly system works. Usually, while the technical director is teaching the crew their jobs, the lighting designer is writing light cues.

The lighting designer, sound designer and director may at some point ask you to go through a series of cues. A true dry tech will include going through the entire show without actors, with you calling the cues and the crew running them. The process for calling cues follows later in this chapter.

> SM TIP: If you are told that your theatre does tech rehearsals with actors, you need to ask if it includes costumes. Sometimes you will do a tech rehearsal one day without costumes and then a second day with costumes.

CUE-TO-CUE TECH

Every once in a while, you will be asked to do a cue-to-cue rehearsal with all tech and actors. This type of technical rehearsal is usually done when there are not a lot of internal cues (cues in the middle of the scenes). When you have completed a sequence (section or grouping) of cues (e.g. the beginning of a scene), you say (using your God mic), "Hold". Then you tell the actors and crew that you will be skipping the dialogue within the scene and jumping to a spot in the script that is approximately a quarter of a page prior to the next sequence of cues. You then make sure the technicians are set for the next sequence of cues and check that the actors are in the correct positions on stage. Once everyone and everything is in place, you will say clearly, "Actor's Go." This makes for a very quick technical rehearsal and helps everyone to focus this rehearsal on the technical aspects.

> SM TIP: If a scene is only a couple of pages long, sometimes it is smarter to let it run rather than to stop and reset. Stopping everything and getting it going again sometimes takes longer than the scene itself. You are the one to determine if the scene is long enough to make the stop.

DRESS TECH

If you are doing a dress tech, you will be doing all the tech with the actors in their costumes. With dress techs the actors may or may not be required to wear stage makeup. That decision is usually made by the director and costume designer. You need to find out when the actors will begin wearing makeup in rehearsals as they will be coming to you to find out.

During a dress tech you will be working all the costume changes as well as the sets and lights and sound. (I will address the organization of costume changes later in this chapter.)

STOP AND GO REHEARSALS

Sometimes you will have a dress rehearsal that is a *stop and go* – meaning, you will rehearse a scene or section, stop when there is a problem, fix it, reset and run that section again. During stop and go rehearsals, if the problem is one that can be fixed by a note or a discussion *after* the rehearsal, you do not stop. But, if it is a sequence of cues that has yet to work without problems during any of the previous rehearsals, and it *still* has problems, stop and rerun it. The decision to stop is made by either the director, a designer, or *you*. It is imperative that you make sure you are comfortable with a sequence of cues during this process before continuing to the next sequence. The next rehearsal will be a dress rehearsal and you don't want to stop if at all possible during it.

DRESS REHEARSALS

Once you have gotten through all the tech rehearsals, you will have a series of dress rehearsals. This means to run through the show with all the tech aspects, without stopping. If you have not rehearsed yet with costumes, this is the time you will do so. Realize that the first time the actors wear costumes, it will take them a little longer to get ready. The first time an actor puts on their completed costume, they will be adjusting it and possibly talking with the costume designer about parts that don't fit exactly right. Instead of taking five minutes to jump into the costume (as it eventually should), it will take 30 minutes for the actor and designer to discuss what "fixes" are needed.

MAKING CHANGES TO RUNNING LISTS

Often, as you are working your way through the technical rehearsals, you will discover a simpler or quicker way to do a change. Make the adjustment. Have everyone note it on their sheets, and, after rehearsal, update the master. After every technical rehearsal you should check with the crew to see if there were any problems or any changes that need to be discussed.

SM EXPERIENCE: The show that had the five actors and numerous costume changes, also had 16 set changes. The running list was 6 pages long. After every tech rehearsal, the crew and I would sit and talk through how to make the show work more efficiently. By our first preview (much to the surprise of the producers), the show *was* running smoothly.

WRITING CUES

The process of writing cues in techs is complicated. You will be given cues from the lighting designer, the sound designer, the tech director and any other persons in charge of an aspect of the show. Write everything down neatly and clearly. If you don't understand when a cue should be called, or the sequence of cues, you need to have it clarified by the person in charge of that aspect.

Carefully and legibly write the cues into your cue script in pencil. Notate the exact word on which the cue should be called. Chose a cueing shorthand for each tech aspect to use in your script. L for "light cue", S for "sound cue", etc. This shorthand has to be clear to other people, just in case you are sick and/or absent from a performance. Most cues will have numbers. (The correct way to "call" each.)

L1 means Light cue one. (Say "lights one")
S1 means Sound cue one. (Say "sound one")
M1 means Music cue one. (Say "music one")
FX1 means special effects one. (Say "F. X. one")
Extra possible notations.
Fly1QL means fly rail one, cue light
TrapQL means trap, cue light
Sometimes a designer (e.g. a sound designer) will give the cues letters. So instead of having S1 you will have SA, etc.
Calling cues will be covered later in this chapter.

> SM TIP: It is very important that you write your cues clearly and neatly. You must make sure that if you are ever absent from a performance, the ASM, the lighting designer, or maybe the director will be able to call the show using your script.

OPENING SEQUENCE OF CUES

Put a blank piece of paper before the first page of your cue script. On this page you can write all the cues that happen *prior* to the show starting. The lighting and sound designers may have pre-show music and lights or "curtain warmers". These cues will be taken *before* the house opens. The sequence of cues prior to the start of the play *may* look like the following:

House Lights go to Half
Announcement made to the audience
Sound starts
House Lights go Out
Stage Lights go Out
Cue the actors to get into place on stage
Stage Lights go Out as Sound fades out

The opening sequence of cues will be determined by the director in consultation with the lighting designer and sound designer. The lighting designer will probably be the one to give you the order of the cues.

> SM TIP: The opening sequence of cues of every show takes longer than any other sequence. Don't start to get frustrated when you approach the one-hour or two-hour mark and you have still not finished the opening section. That is not unusual.

LIGHTING CUES

The lighting designer may have put some cues into the light board prior to the technical rehearsals, and then, they will be showing the director the cues. At the same time, the lighting designer will be giving you the placement of the cues for your script.

Most times the lighting designer will have written the cues in their script prior to the dry tech. Some times they will let the stage manager sit with the script a day before dry tech in order to transfer the cues and their numbers into the cue script. This is ideal, because you will have time in a less stressful moment to write the cues into your script. Don't expect the lighting designer to have time prior to the techs to clarify any of the cues. That will be done during the dry tech or the dress tech. Always note any questions you might have about the placement of a cue, so that you check with the lighting designer for clarification. Sometimes the lighting designer will let you take their script with cues home with you so that you can write them into your script at your own pace, but don't depend on this. Usually, you are sitting in the theatre as lights are being focused.

PLACEMENT OF CUES IN SCRIPT

The notation of cues in your script is similar to the notation of blocking in your prompt script. The lighting designer will put cues in the middle of lines, before lines start (anticipation), after lines, and on a designated syllable in the middle of a six syllable word. Notate each cue carefully.

If the lighting designer specifies a light cue for a particular part of a line of dialogue, e.g. "At the *beginning* of this line…" place a hash mark (/) at the beginning of that line and underline the line of dialogue during which the cue takes place extending it to the edge of the page. You will then write the cue type (e.g. Lights or Sound) and the cue number on the line outside the text.

HARRY
/How do you know I took the paper?   *L11*

If the designer says, "At the *end* of this line…" then you would place the hash mark after the last word of that line and draw your line once again to the edge of the page.

HARRY
How do you know I took the paper?/   *L11*

If the designer says, "Somewhere around here…" then you don't make a hash mark, you just write the cue in the margins by the line or paragraph they mention.

HARRY

How do you know I took the paper?   _L11_

Sometimes the lighting designer will be as specific as saying, "On this syllable…" In this case, you need to put a hash mark before the syllable.

HARRY

How do you know I took the pa/per?   _L11_

Write the cues outside the text. When you turn each page of the script, you can easily see when the next cue is.

WRITING SOUND CUES

The sound designer may give you a list of the sound cues complete with what the sound is and when it happens. More often you will get the cues and the corresponding numbers/letters as you go through the tech rehearsal process. You should write the sound cues using the same style that I presented in writing light cues.

Sometimes, the designer will have cues which dictate the sound to fade down - not out - then another cue to bring the sound back up again. This can happen if you are doing a show that calls for background sound (e.g. crickets) and they need to be louder and more obvious at certain points. Instead of the sound board operator figuring this out on their own, it should be written as a cue which the stage manager "calls".

CUES THAT DO NOT HAPPEN ON LINES

You know what to do when you have a cue that is supposed to happen on a line of dialogue. When it is a "visual cue" (meaning the cue happens on a characters move), you should note it on the line that you draw.

(When Harry reaches the door)   **L13**
_____

When the cue happens on a sound, note that.

(Third ring of the phone)   **L14**
_____

Sometimes you will be given a "clear" from your ASM. (e.g. when you cannot see an actor exit, and the ASM has to tell your that they are off stage).

(When ASM says actor is clear)   **L15**
_____

Whatever the cue is, you need to note it clearly in your script.

SIMULTANEOUS CUES

    Many times you will have two or more cues that need to happen simultaneously. When you are writing them in your cue script you need to put a bracket { around the cues that go together.

   …things./   { **L6**
                        SG

MULTIPLE CUES

    Often you will have a quick sequence of cues. Each cue should have it's own cue line noted and be separated from the others.

   …things./   **L7**
      (on "complete")   **SH**
   (10 seconds into music)   **L8**

NOTATING OTHER INFORMATION

    Remember when writing the cues in your script to keep it neat. Write down *all* the information that you need in order to understand when the cue happens, and what the sequence should look or sound like. So the cues above would now look like this.

...things./   *(blackout)*   *L7*
    (on "complete" start "Your Smile")   *SH*
(10 seconds into music: lights up in hall)   *L8*

> SM TIP: Don't fall into the trap of thinking, "I'll remember where to take this cue." After a long day's technical rehearsal, you will be lucky to remember the name of the show. Write everything down.

CUE LIGHTS

Sometimes you will have a box in the booth that has toggle switches which control cue lights backstage. These cue lights are used to communicate with a crew member who is not on a headset. For this example, I will use the crew member who is stationed at the fly rail. This is how it works: you shift the fly rail toggle switch into the "on" position (turning the light at the fly rail *on*); the fly rail crew member is now in *standby* mode; once the cue word is spoken by the actor on stage, you shift the toggle switch into the "off" position (turning the light at the fly rail *off*); the crew member sees the light go off and performs their assigned job at that moment (e.g. raising a drop).

> SM TIP: It is suggested that there are two lights at the end of each line for cue lights. That way if one bulb burns out during a show, you still have the second bulb.
> ANOTHER SM TIP: If you have several cue lights in close proximity, they should be different colors. Then, the fly rail person won't mistakenly lower a drop when another crew person is supposed to be pulling a set piece off the stage.

STANDBY

In your cue script, you need to write a "standby" for all your cues. This is the warning to the crew that they have a specific cue or series of cues coming up. Once you have written all the sound and light cues in your script, go through it again and write the standby for every cue. The standby should be 5-6 lines (maximum) before the actual cue. Don't put them so far ahead that the crew member is waiting too long (like having the light board op hold their finger over the go button for so long, the finger starts to shake). You may be able to write in the standbys as you go through the writing of cues with the designers. If there are a lot of cues, and there is no time to write the standbys in during the tech, then you must write them in on a break between rehearsals.

Write your standbys in the right hand margin of the script. Do *not* underline them (as you did the actual cue). You want them to stand out, but not as much as the cue itself. You can use a shorthand for standby (e.g. sby). A single cue would look like this:

Sby L7

If you have a sequence of cues, you will need to standby the entire sequence. You will do this when there is not enough time between cues to give a standby to the board ops.

Sby

L7 & 8

SH

When you are telling the crew to standby, always say the word standby first so as not to confuse a standby with an actual cue. For example: "Standby Lights 7 and 8 and Sound H".

CUEING SCRIPT EXAMPLE
What follows is a page of the *Some Sweet Day* cue script. Transition from Act One, Scene Five, Fob's House to Scene Six, the Church: Fob's house flies out and the church flies in. The cue script key is as follows:
QL2 = Cue Light for Church Door (to Fly in or out)
QL3 = Cue Light for Fob's House (to Fly in or out)
QL5 = Cue Light SR for actors
QL6 = Cue Light SL for actors.
TPOQ = Turn Page Over Quickly (cues coming)
Ø = out

You say, "Standby Lights 38, 39, and 40" and turn the toggle switches for cue lights 2, 3, 5, and 6 "on" at the same time.

FOB
You better go on in and eat. It's late.

WILLETHA
Aren't you going to come in with me?

FOB

Standby:
L38,39,40
QL 2&3 ON
QL 5&6 ON

I think I'll stay out here a little longer.

WILLETHA
Well, don't be too long. When you were rubbing my shoulders, it reminded me of what you said to Isaac the other day.

FOB
What was that?

WILLETHA
(Smiles) "Practice makes perfect."

FOB
Oh, yeah?

WILLETHA
Uh huh. And you've got a long way to go.
(She exits. / Fob follows.) *(visual)*

L38
QL2&3 Ø

as Fob off stage

L39
QL5&6Ø

TPOQ

As Willetha exits, you say, "Lights 38 Go" and turn the toggle switch for Cue lights 2 & 3 off simultaneously. Then as Fob is off stage, say, "Lights 39 Go" and turn the toggle switches for cue lights 5 & 6 off, simultaneously. Immediately, turn the page over. And on the second knock, say, "Lights 40 Go".

SCENE SIX
(The scene returns to the Full Gospel Church. Sarah Jane is preparing for the meeting. As the members arrive, they give the union knock and password. The knock is: knock, knock, pause, knock. The password is: "What time is it?" with a response of "It's not too late." Some members are already in the church.)

(A <u>knock is heard.</u>)   *(after 2ⁿᵈ knock)*   L40

SARAH JANE
What time is it?

MAE
(From outside.) It's not too late.

SETTING SOUND LEVELS

As you work through the tech, the sound designer will have the sound board operator adjust the volume levels of the sound cues. When this happens, you may have to use the God mic to quiet the whole theatre.

Sometimes, prior to the tech, the sound designer and the director will set aside time to listen and set levels for the cues. You need to be present and the theatre needs to be quiet during this session.

Throughout the tech process, the sound designer will be making adjustments to the levels and the cue lines for the sound cues. Keep checking during the techs to make sure no cue lines are altered or new cues added.

WORKING THROUGH SET CHANGES

Each crew member should be given a copy of the final running list, as well as a separate list of their individual cues.

1) During the technical rehearsal, when you get to the point in the play just prior to a set change, stop the actors ("Hold").

2) Over the God mic, tell everyone the steps to the set change.

3) Ask if anyone has any questions.

4) If it is a complicated change, have the actors step to the front of the stage or into the house and watch, while the crew runs the change. (By seeing it first, they will not be surprised by a house flying in behind them as they exit the scene.)

5) Reset and do the set change again, with the actors giving their lines and or entering/exiting.

6) Once you have talked through any changes, you reset, and this time through, add lights and sound.

After each of these steps you need to ask everyone involved if they have any questions or comments: the technical director might want to have the fly crew run something in quicker or slower; the director might want to tell an actor to wait for the house to come all the way in, before making their entrance; or an actor might ask if they could exit after the set piece has started to fly out.

Once the sequence is completed, you may choose to do it again. There are only four people who can request that you go back and redo a sequence: the director, the designers, the technical director, and you yourself.

> SM TIP: If you do not feel secure in calling a sequence, it is very important that you speak up and let it be known that you want to run it again. Often, set changes have to be run again and again to get everything coordinated correctly. Don't panic. It will come together.

Sometimes, you will have an assistant whose job it will be to "run the deck". Together, go over all the change sheets, so that they can talk the crew through the changes. In this way, two things are happening at once. While you are writing cues with the lighting designer and director, the ASM is working with the running crew to organize the deck. If you do *not* have an ASM, you will be running back and forth. It is more time consuming, but all the work has to happen: cue by cue, set change by set change.

ORGANIZING QUICK CHANGES

The procedure for organizing a quick costume change during tech is similar to that used for set changes.

1) During the technical rehearsal, when you are approaching a cueing sequence that includes a quick change, stop the actors ("Hold").

2) Over the God mic, tell everyone that the quick change needs to be teched.

3) Talk through the quick change with the actor and the wardrobe person to determine the sequence to the costume change: who takes off what piece of clothing first, who helps with the next piece, what the actor can do on their own, what they need help with. (The actor and the wardrobe person or costume designer may have already figured out the steps.

4) Run the costume change without lights, with the actors giving their lines and or entering/exiting, while you watch it to make sure it is running smoothly.

5) Ask if anyone has any questions or suggestions for making the change smoother.

6) Reset and do the change again, adding: the lines, entrances/exits, sound, and lights.

This time through tell everyone not to stop unless there is a problem. Afterwards, see if the actor and the wardrobe person are secure before you continue with the next section of the show. It is best to take the time during techs to make sure the changes work. Sometimes, there will be fixes to the change that can be done with a discussion afterwards. When you get to the dress rehearsals, if a change is still causing problems, you should tech it again *before* starting the dress rehearsal, so you don't have to stop *during* it.

CALLING CUES

When calling cues always use a clear voice and enunciate. You must speak with authority. Don't hesitate and don't second guess yourself. By the time you get to dress rehearsals, you will feel like you know when each cue is given.

When calling cues you always say "Go" as the cue for the person performing the cue. They have been trained or told to listen for you to say their job and "Go" (e.g. "Lights: Go.") You say "Go" *with* the last syllable of the last word in the cue line. By saying the "Go" with the last syllable, the cue will begin immediately after the line. If you say the "Go", after the last syllable, then there is a slight delay between the end of the line and the beginning of the cue.

SINGLE CUE

The process for a single cue is as follows:
Give the standby for the cue
"Standby Lights 9"
The light board operator responds
"Lights standing by"
Then as the cue nears say
"Lights 9 GO."

SIMULTANEOUS CUES

If you have simultaneous cues (ones that happen on the same cue word) the process is:
Give standbys for all cues to follow
"Standby Lights 9 and Sound A"
The light and sound board operators respond
"Lights standing by." and
"Sound standing by."
Then as the cue nears say
"Lights 9 and Sound A GO."

MULTIPLE CUES
If you have a sequence that doesn't have time for standbys *between* cues, you need to work the *whole sequence*. The process is:
> Give standbys for the *whole sequence*
> > "Standby Lights 9, 10 and 11, and
> > Sound A and B"
> The light and sound board operators respond
> > "Lights standing by." and
> > "Sound standing by."
> Then as the sequence nears the first cue
> > "Lights 9 and Sound A GO"
> the next cue comes up quickly
> > "Lights 10 GO
> the final cue comes
> > "Lights 11 and Sound B GO"

SM TIP: NEVER SAY "GO" FIRST. If you say "Go Lights 1" the board operator won't know when to actually push the button. You have to train yourself to give the cues in a style that is consistent. There should be no pauses in calling a cue. This is one of the hardest aspects for novice stage managers to grasp. Don't get disheartened. Remember, the actors have had weeks or months to learn their parts. You get a couple of days. By the time you get to final dress, you will feel like it is easy. (Maybe not easy, but easier.)

SPECIAL NOTES ON CALLING CUES
Sometimes you will have such a quick sequence that you will not be able to say all of the words. The process then is:
> Give standbys for the whole sequence
> > "Standby Lights 9, 10 and 11, and
> > Sound A and B"
> The light and sound board operators respond
> > "Lights standing by" and
> > "Sound standing by"

Then you add
"This is a tight sequence I will just be saying
        Lights and Sound after the first cues"
Then as the sequence nears the first cue
"Lights 9 and Sound A GO"
immediately
"Lights GO"
immediately
"Lights and Sound GO"

Sometimes you don't even have time to say anything and you will just be saying "GO...GO...GO". If it is a follow cue where the sound starts a moment after the lights you might just say "Lights 9 Go, Sound Go".

SM TIP: Sometimes, you have to rely on the light board op or another crew member to give you a "complete" when their move/cue is finished. This happens when you cannot see or hear the completion of a cue, and need to call the "go" for another cue when the first is completed. Put into your cue script with the standby, a note to re-mind the crew member to say "complete".

HEADSET ETIQUETTE
        Some headset etiquette is common sense. As there are always several people on them, idle talk must be kept to a minimum. During technical rehearsals, there is a lot of discussion on headset (light and sound cues, as well as, the SM and ASM conversing about set changes, for example). Sometimes the lighting personnel (lighting designer, master electrician, and follow spot operators) will be on a separate channel, so that they can talk to each other without disrupting the stage manager.

HEADSET RULES
        1) There is no talking on the headset between a "standby" and a cue.

2) No one except the stage manager should *leave* head-
    set microphones turned on. Everyone else should
    turn them on to talk, and then, immediately, turn
    them off again when they are done with the conver-
    sation. If the headset mic is in the *on* position and a
    person accidentally hits it with their hand, it is very
    loud and painful in the ears of the others on headset.
    If the mic is in the *off* position when this happens, it
    won't bust everyone's eardrums.

3) If someone has to take their headset off for any rea-
    son, they should inform the stage manager that they
    are "going off headset." When they return, they
    need to listen to make sure you are not in the middle
    of a sequence of cues, and then say "back on head-
    set".

4) Idle chatter is not allowed on the headsets. Your job
    is to keep an eye on the show. If you are talking
    about a movie, a class, or a party, you are not doing
    the job that you have been given.

MOVING INTO THE BOOTH

During tech rehearsals, you will be seated in the audience at the tech table. When you get to dress rehearsals (that are
not stop and go), you should move your station into the booth. It
will have a different feel than the tech table: you will see the
stage from a different angle, you will see the stage through glass,
you will be listening to the actors through a small speaker, and
the angle of your view of the stage will be different. You need to
have *at least* two dress rehearsals calling the show from the
booth.

PART FOUR

PERFORMANCES

CHAPTER NINE

☑RUNNING THE SHOW

You will be arriving at the theatre one to one and a half hours before the curtain. During this time, you will be getting yourself and everyone else ready for the show. Everyone will have their assigned jobs, but it is your responsibility to make sure they complete them.

> SM TIP: Once the technical rehearsals are completed and you are now "running" the show in performance, leave your cueing script in a secure location, usually the booth. If you happen to miss a performance, it should be available to the person replacing you.

SHOW CHECK LISTS

In order to make the routine of running a show as uncomplicated as possible, organize a preshow and a post show checklist. You will carry these lists with you before and after the show to check off every duty that you must perform.

A preshow checklist might include:

Calls
Light check
Sound check
Backstage overhead (flourescent) lights off
Backstage blues on
Props set on stage
Props set on table

It will include anything that you must do before the show. Even turning your cell phone off should be included. Include jobs that are specific to a theatre (e.g. taping the backstage door so it doesn't slam). These lists will help you when there is a "problem" before a show and you get distracted from your *normal* routine. You won't forget to do something if you are in the habit of checking it off the list.

The post show checklist is often the reverse of the preshow list, where items like, turn *on* backstage blues will now say turn *off* backstage blues. It also often includes:

Valuables returned

Booth locked

"Ghost light" on

Dressing Room picked up

Props in prop cabinet

This would include special aspects of your theatre (e.g. take the tape off the backstage door, so it locks).

Don't be afraid of going too far in making your lists. Better that it is on a list, than forgotten.

THE PRESHOW ROUTINE

Before each performance, the stage and backstage need to be swept. You can assign this to an ASM or a crew person. After sweeping, they should go over the area with a damp mop. (The mop should not be soaking wet, just damp enough to pick up the dust.) Discuss with the technical director or set designer the best way to take care of the deck.

Props should be set on stage, on prop tables, or wherever they need to be for the top of the show. Again, an ASM or crew person could be assigned this job. There is nothing worse for an actor than being on stage and having a costume or prop missing or set incorrectly.

The lighting and sound board operators are responsible for sound and light checks. Check with both to ensure they have completed their tasks. Don't let them wait until five minutes before the house opens to do this. At that time, if there is a problem, it will hold up opening the house and possibly the show.

SM TIP: When working in the professional theatre, you will find a lot of actors check their props before the show. I recommend this for any production.

TIME TO OPEN THE HOUSE

Once the light and sound board operators have done their checks, they should turn on the preshow lights and music, if necessary. Tell the cast when the "House" is opening, so they won't be tempted to walk out on the stage for any last-minute matters. Then, find the house manager and let them know that the stage and actors are ready for the house to open.

WORKING WITH THE HOUSE MANAGER

Each theatre has its own peculiarities as far as house management is concerned. The following are the norms when working with a house manager. Make sure, before the first performance for an audience, that you meet with the house manager and discuss the house procedures.

Besides letting the house manager know when the stage is set for the house to open, you also have to deal with late arrivals in the audience. Check in with the house manager at five minutes to curtain, and find out if there are any groups that are running late. Prior to the first public performance, discuss with the director when latecomers can be seated. Usually, it is after the first scene of the show. That only works for smaller groups of latecomers. If a large group is late, you might want to hold the curtain for them, so that the audience, and the actors, are not distracted when they enter. Protocol regarding holding the curtain for a group, is something that the producer, director, and house manager decide.

Some box offices have a headset so that the house manager can communicate to the stage manager. Other theatres rely on a "thumbs up" from the house manager when the house is ready and the doors are closed. The important thing is that you are communicating.

GIVING CALLS

It is one of your primary responsibilities to let the actors and crew know how much time they have before curtain. It is standard in the theatre to give "thirty minutes", "fifteen minutes", "five minutes" and "places" calls. Everyone should respond with a "thank you". If they don't, remind them that it is proper theatre etiquette and that you need to make sure they heard you. (If they don't respond to "fifteen minutes", you may find an actor crazed when you give "five minutes", and they realize there is not enough time left for them to get ready). When you give calls to the cast and crew, it is also an ideal opportunity for them to ask you questions (such as what day the photo call is going to be).

You also give a "house open" call and at intermission, you give "ten minutes", "five minutes" and "places".

SM TIP: Often theatres have a microphone in the booth and backstage for making announcements to the dressing rooms or green room. I would not use this as the normal way to give calls: the actors may not hear or acknowledge you. A face-to-face call is much better. Sometimes, it is necessary to give the "places" call over the microphone, because the light booth is far from backstage. (In that situation, the ASM should be on headset backstage to tell you when the actors are in place.

SIGN IN SHEET

The sign in sheet is now more important than ever. If the actors' call is an hour before curtain, at that time you need to check to see if everyone has signed in. If they have not signed in, then you have to determine if they are late or just *forgot* to sign in. Ask the other cast members if they have seen the "missing actor". If they have not, call the actor on their phone. If they *have* seen them, then you have to go on an "actor hunt". In a small theatre with only a few cast members, this is not very difficult. But, if it is a large theatre and a large show, you could spend ten to fifteen minutes trying to find an actor. Remind the actors that at call time, they should stay in the backstage area: you may have to put on an understudy, so you need the entire cast where you can find them. Don't let the actors sign each other in. It is a very bad habit with potential problems for you.

VALUABLES

Although everyone on a show is part of a "big family", it is still advisable to lock up "valuables" during performances. An actor may be married, but their character may not be. They might not want to leave their wedding ring or engagement ring lying around.

Large manila envelopes with an actor's name written on each one usually works well for storing personal items. At the first dress rehearsal, distribute the envelopes. Then, before every dress rehearsal and performance, as you are giving either "fifteen mintues" or "thirty minutes", you can collect their valuables. It is the actor's choice if they want to put anything into the envelope for you to collect. Valuables should be locked up during the show in a safe place. Sometimes this is an office, other times it might be the locking drawer in a desk.

SM EXPERIENCE: I once did a tour in West Virginia to high schools and middle schools. Because we were touring, we did not have an office in which to lock up valuables. I would put them on the stage inside a platform. No one could steal them from there, as three or four hundred people were always watching.

After the show is over, the first thing you need to do is to return the valuables back to the actors. They can then leave the envelope with their makeup and will have it available for the next show.

MONITORS

Hopefully, the theatre has sound and/or video monitors backstage, so the actors can see/hear what is happening on the stage. With a monitor, they can tell when they are needed on the stage. If the theatre does not have a monitor system, you can either spend lots of time asking your ASM to go get actors for their scenes, or you can invest in a baby monitor. If you get a baby monitor, buy one with two receivers. Hide the monitor on the stage where it won't be in the actor's way, and put the receivers in the dressing rooms. Put on your preshow check list to turn them on, and your post show check list to turn them off. Otherwise, you run through a lot of batteries.

PRESHOW ANNOUNCEMENTS
       The theatre may have a recorded announcement that is used during performances. If they don't, you may be called upon to read the announcement before the show. Remember to enunciate and talk at a comfortable pace. The information you are giving the audience is very important.

WATCHING THE SHOW
       During the show while you are calling cues, you will also be keeping an eye on the show itself. Watch the actors and make sure they are not making changes in the movement or the lines. Until you start working in the professional theatre, the director will probably be at all performances and taking notes. If the director is not present, it is your job to make sure that the show stays the same as they envisioned it. Sometimes you have to tell the actors to take out their "improvements".

SM EXPERIENCE: Once, I realized that an actor was having trouble speaking (the audience was not aware of the problem). I knew that she would not be leaving the stage for the next two scenes, except for a moment during the set change. I told the ASM to have a glass of water for her at that moment. At intermission, the actor said, "Thank you", and told me she was impressed that I had noticed. Because I had carefully been watching her performance for weeks, I could tell she was having some kind of a problem.

While watching the show, you will also note if there are any problems with the set , lights, props, or costumes (e.g. a light is no longer the color it was when you opened the show). These notes will become part of the "performance report". Give the notes to the crew person in charge of that aspect.

AFTER THE SHOW

Immediately go backstage with the valuables, in case an actor is leaving the theatre quickly. Make any announcements as you return the valuables (e.g. the next day's call). If there is a rehearsal call or a matinee, you need to make sure you remind them of the earlier call time. You can give the actors notes from the performance as they are getting out of costume and makeup.

SM TIP: If you are working in an area where, in the spring, you switch to Daylight Saving Time, don't forget to remind the actors and the crew to turn their clocks forward. You don't want to have an actor miss a show because they forgot to change their clock.

As with your preshow routine, you need to make sure that the crew has performed their jobs. Your post show checklist will help you to make sure nothing is overlooked. Sometimes you are responsible for locking the backstage door, so you must be the last one out.

Your post show duties will vary from theatre to theatre. Find out what you will be responsible for, so that you can complete your job.

PERFORMANCE REPORT

After every perfomance you will write a report with the pertinent notes from that show that will be distributed to the producer, the director, the production manager, designers, and crew heads. The report will include the times for the show, whether there were problems, actors who were late or absent, understudies, and if there were any special rehearsals that day. You will include any notes that you took during the course of the show, and information on any accidents that may have happened.

A Survival Guide for Stage Managers

As with the rehearsal report, email the performance report immediately after the show. If there are notes that someone needs to attend to, follow up the next day to see if it has been accomplished.

PERFORMANCE REPORT   4/12/07

SOME SWEET DAY

8:11   Curtain Up
9:16   Intermission
9:31   Begin Act Two
10:12   Curtain Down
Reason for curtain hold:
        Act One--Latecomers
Running Time: 2 hours 1 minute
        Act One   1 hour 5 minutes
        Act Two   41 minutes
Audience: Full House
        Standing Ovation

ACTORS:
        Understudies:
        Show Notes:
                Jessup was out of light in Woods
        Accidents:

TECHNICAL NOTES:
        SET
        COSTUMES
        LIGHTS
        PROPS
        SOUND—Clea's body mics didn't work

NEXT PERFORMANCE:
        Friday, April 13 at 8:00 pm
CALL: 6:30 FOR CAST AND CREW

CHAPTER TEN

☑SPECIAL SITUATIONS

The following are some special situations that you may encounter in your future as a stage manager and stories of situations that I encountered and how I dealt with them.

STAGE COMBAT

Many shows have some form of combat—either slaps or fights or swordplay. Hopefully, your theatre has hired a fight director to teach safe techniques to the actors. Your job will be to schedule combat rehearsals and attend them the way you would any other rehearsal. Once the show opens, you need to make sure that the actors involved in combat run the fight sequences (sections of the play that include combat) every night before the show (the fight captain is in charge of these). Because you are responsible for how every performance goes, it is very important to keep an eye on the combat for safety reasons. You don't want to have to replace an actor because of an injury.

The more you understand about stage combat the better. Members of the Society of American Fight Directors (SAFD) offer classes all around the country for combatants in hand-to-hand, broadsword, quarterstaff, as well as sword and dagger. The teachers are highly trained and stress the importance of safety in combat. You can find them on the Internet.

SM EXPERIENCE: While working on the outdoor drama, *Tecumseh*, I took my first combat workshop through the SAFD. For six weeks, I learned the basics of hand-to-hand, quarterstaff, and rapier & dagger. I have used the knowledge learned during that course (and subsequent ones) in numerous shows.

PYROTECHNICS/SMOKE/FIRE

Explosions, flashes and smoke are technical aspects that you must deal with every "once in a while". Whenever there are explosions, hopefully a pyrotechnician will be hired. That is not always the case, as theatres will often just use the local "magic shop" for their pyrotechnic needs. As the stage manager, you must be diligent in making sure that everyone involved is safe. If you are calling cues for explosions, you must be very aware that they need to be teched the same way everything else is: very carefully. During runs (techs or performances), you need to be "in sync" with where all the actors are at any moment, when an explosion is about to occur. Common sense dictates that if an actor seems too close to the point of explosion, then you do not give the "go" to the pyrotechnician. It may be a cliché, but, it *is* better to be safe than sorry.

If smoke is being used in the show, be aware that it is very hard to manipulate. Smoke machines usually have to "warm up". This may cause a delay in terms of when you call the cue, and when you actually see the smoke on the stage. In addition, smoke will continue to rise *after* you have called the cue that stops the machine. It may take several rehearsals for you, the designers, and the technical director to get the perfect cue line, so the director gets the visual scene onstage that they want.

If the show includes fire, the technical director will address fire codes and fireproofing issues. For you, it is a matter of making sure that you know the safety procedure being used and the safety mechanisms incorporated.

All of these matters involve the technical director and possibly the fire marshal for the theatre.

MUSICALS

Most of this book applies to working on a musical. The only *real* difference between a musical and a straight play is that in a musical there are more things to organize, more people to organize, and music to accompany it all. Having said that, here are several areas of a musical production that must be considered.

REHEARSAL PIANIST/PIANO

Sometimes the music director will play the piano during rehearsals. Other times, the theatre will hire a rehearsal pianist. In either situation, music rehearsals should be treated the same as acting rehearsals. Prepare what is needed (e.g. chairs, music stands) and take notes throughout.

> SM TIP: Some people may say that listening to singers learn songs is boring. I think it is a great *opportunity* to get familiar with every beat of the show. Remember, the lighting designer will be placing cues throughout the songs. The better you know the music, the easier it will be when you have to call those cues.

BAND/ORCHESTRA REHEARSALS

In the beginning of the rehearsal process, band or orchestra rehearsals are held separate from the acting rehearsals. Eventually, you will schedule a "sitzprobe": a seated rehearsal for the band and performers to go through the music in the entire show together.

The sitzprobe (literally "seat rehearsal" in German) is usually held in a rehearsal hall. Because it is the first time the actors and the band are playing together, it can be a slow process. The music director will want to work through the music from the first number to the last. If there are problems, a number will be repeated, until it is working correctly. Remind everyone, to bring "patience" with them.

SM TIP: The sitzprobe is one of the most exciting rehearsals. Everyone is hearing the "show" for the first time. It is also another *opportunity* for you (before tech starts). The music will sound different with the band and you may not have the cast and band together again, until dress rehearsals.

BAND EQUIPMENT

Make sure the band's rehearsal space has everything they need: music stands, chairs of different heights for different instruments, and electrical outlets. You also need to check that the overhead lighting in the space is adequate for them to read their music.

PIT OR ON STAGE

Whether the band is in the pit or on the stage for the actual performances will affect a number of issues. This decision should be made early in the process by the director, producer and set designer.

If the band is on the stage, they may be in costume. Then, you will have to organize fittings for them as well. You may have to deal with procuring music stands or chairs that are different from what you are using in rehearsal (e.g. music stands that fit in a period piece). You will have to keep an eye on the music stand lights: they can get turned in the wrong direction and shine in the audience's eyes. Be aware of everything that will relate to them throughout the performance. If you notice a band/orchestra member has changed their set up, or is wearing a different shirt during the show, you need to note that in your performance report and then talk to the person about it.

If the band is in a pit, then they will probably be required to wear black or dark clothing. You will need to check a lot of the same issues: lighting, stands and chairs.

Whether on stage or in the pit, additional issues are: can the conductor see the actors; can the actors see the conductor; and does the conductor need a cue light for the top of the acts as well as for any other cues that you give them.

MICROPHONES

Most musicals are done with microphones. Before every performance, the sound operator needs to do mic checks. It is your job to make sure the actors are ready when needed. If the band is mic'ed, you need to find out if they need to do mic checks. You need a backup plan in case a mic goes out during the show. This will vary, but needs to be discussed *before* it happens.

TECHNICAL REHEARSALS/DRESS REHEARSALS

Relatively early in the rehearsal process the decision needs to be made concerning which rehearsals the band will be attending. Often, the band will have separate rehearsals and will not come into the process until the end of the technical rehearsals. Once you know when the band is required, give them the correct dates and times. There should only be one person giving them their call times, and that person should be the stage manager. Otherwise, somewhere along the line you will end up minus a band member or two for a rehearsal. A friendly reminder, a few days before their first call with the cast, is not a bad idea.

CALLING MUSICALS

I've seen people call musicals who can't read music, but they understand the process of calling cues, and they have become very familiar with the music. Usually, you will have many more cues for a musical than most plays. Be very specific when you are writing the cues in your cue script. Most cues will not be on the music, but on a word of the lyrics. If a cue is on a specific beat of the music, familiarize yourself with that part of the music.

MISCELLANEOUS

Although it is not in your "jurisdiction" you may be called on to schedule a piano tuning. Even if you are not the one scheduling it, the music director will often ask that you make sure it happens.

WORKING WITH CHILDREN

Whenever there are children in a show, it is the stage manager's job to make sure their parents know the schedule and work involved. Beyond that, you have to be aware of how they are interacting with the rest of the company. You are not a baby-sitter, but sometimes, you need to arrange for that type of service. If you are doing a show with children, you might need to ask the parents to take turns staying with the kids backstage during rehearsals and performances. You can ask a parent to be the organizer, to set up a schedule. This way, during rehearsals and performances, you won't be spending your time trying to keep the children controlled.

SM EXPERIENCE: Having been a child actor, I know that a lot of people watched out for me. As I got older and became a teenager, it bothered me that so many people were watching what I was doing. As I look back, I am very happy that others were keeping an eye on me, as it kept me from getting in *too much* trouble. As a stage manager, I have always kept a close eye on any younger members of the company. A few years ago, an actor came up to me on the first day of rehearsal. We had done a show together when he was 8 years old. He remembered me (in a good way) because I had taken time to get to know him and "watched out for him".

WORKING WITH ANIMALS

Sometimes, you have to work with animals: a dog, a cat, or a horse. Usually, there is someone whose job it is to take care of the animal. The theatre may have hired a trained dog, or, the director's girlfriend is letting you use "Fluffy". If "Fluffy" is in the show, someone has to be responsible for taking care of her needs (e.g. walks, water). If it is delegated to several people, some time in the future there will be a problem. Make sure to have *one* person responsible for this job.

If you choose to work in outdoor theatre (a great learn-ing situation for stage managers), you will often deal with horses. Most theatres have an equestrian or two, whose sole job is to take care of the horses. You will be scheduling riding lessons for the actors, and possibly, scheduling people to help take care of them. Sometimes, *you* will be the one who has to scoop the poop (a story I won't share).

UNDERSTUDIES

Most non-professional shows will not require the stage manager to "work in" understudies. If there are understudies, the director will deal with it. In a professional theatre, it *is* the stage manager's job. If you have kept up to date and precise in your prompt script, you should be able to give the blocking to the actor. Pay close attention to the director during rehearsals. You must know what they are thinking about each character, so you can share it with the understudy. You need to always be prepared to put an understudy into the show.

PHOTO SHOOTS

Most theatres will want to take photos of the shows for publicity and posterity. You will work with the director and the person doing the publicity to set these up.

PUBLICITY SHOOT

Sometimes, a newspaper photographer will attend a rehearsal to get "action" shots for the local paper. Usually, these take very little time, as the photographer will work around what happens during rehearsal (i.e. no "set" shots). At other times, the photographer will want a "directing" shot with actors and director. This will take a little longer as the rehearsal has to stop in order to accomplish this.

PHOTO SHOOT (For posterity)

The director will make a list of 15-20 shots of the show they wish to have photographed and give you the list. Organize them starting with the *end* of the show and proceeding to the *beginning*. This will help cut down the amount of time for the actors to change costumes, as you will start with the costume they have on at the end of the show. (Usually, this photo shoot is held after a performance.) When scheduling the picture order, a picture with one to three actors, can often be scheduled while other actors are changing into a different costume. Looking for any instance where you can be taking one picture while actors are changing for the next picture, will help to move the shoot along quickly. A typed list of the order of shots should be distributed to the director and photographer, as well as posted backstage for the actors.

Go through the order of shots noting which light cues are used, and which set pieces are needed. Give the crew members, who are involved, a copy of *this* list. The more organized you are, the faster the shoot will go. Everyone will be grateful.

REIMBURSEMENTS

Some theatres will give you a stage management budget. This money is used to purchase things needed for the show. Possibly, it is for coffee and donuts at the first rehearsal. It varies from theatre to theatre.

You will be expected to turn in receipts for any expenses. The theatre will have a reimbursement voucher that they use. If they don't supply the voucher, you will need to attach each receipt to a letter size piece of paper and number them. Then, on a separate piece of paper: list the number of each receipt, the vendor listed on the receipt, the amount of money to be reimbursed, the article bought, and the purpose of the article. At the bottom of the page, or the last page, you should note the total amount of money to be reimbursed. Make sure to make a copy of all your receipts, and the cover sheet for your records, *before* you give the originals to the theatre.

PART FIVE

THE CAREER

CHAPTER ELEVEN

☑PURSUING A CAREER

There is not a perfect way to pursue a career in stage management. If you speak to three professional stage managers, they will have three different stories as to how they got to where they are. The following might help you organize yourself, and lead you toward a successful career.

In order to have a career in stage management, you need to base it in an interdisciplinary approach to theatre. You can do this by working your way through the professional theatre (e.g. an internships) or by going to college (most professional stage managers have at least a bachelors degree in theatre.)

THE COLLEGE EXPERIENCE

It doesn't have to be the perfect college, or the biggest. The experience is what *you* put into it. As I said in an earlier chapter, take classes in all areas of the theatre process, including: acting, directing, dance, music, and all the technical areas. Work on as many shows as possible, doing different types of jobs on them. If you only stage manage one show a semester, then, make sure to work as a light board or sound board operator, or running crew on another show. Get some experience in all areas of technical theatre—lights, sets, costumes, props, etc. Try to work with as many different directors as possible, as this will help you enormously when working in the professional theatre.

GRADUATE SCHOOL
Many graduate schools need a stage manager in their theatre program. Some of them are associated with professional theatres. Graduate assistantships and financial aid are available, so that it does not have to be exorbitantly expensive. A word of warning—don't decide that there is only one graduate school that you can attend. The bigger programs are very competitive. Just because the school is large, doesn't mean it is better. There are a lot of good programs *throughout* the country. Talk to your school faculty for suggestions. Get online, check out schools, and then, go see them.

URTA
The University/Resident Theatre Association (URTA) holds auditions/interviews every January. Graduate schools and professional theatres from around the country attend, to find potential theatre people, including stage managers. URTA has a complete website with all the information you would need regarding their association.

PROFESSIONAL THEATRE INTERNSHIPS
Most professional theatres have websites where you can find out information on stage management internships. You can look at local theatres where you currently live, or you can look at theatres around the country. Check each out carefully. Do they pay? Do they offer housing? Some offer a weekly stipend *and* housing. Others don't offer anything. Is it an Equity theatre? Pay careful attention to the possibility of future work after your internship or assistantship is completed.

Every major metropolitan area has at least one professional theatre with an internship program. New York City is full of them, but they don't offer housing. Some of them do pay stipends and many of them will offer college credit.

SUMMER THEATRES
There are numerous professional theatres around the country that offer summer work for theatre students. There are organizations like the Southeastern Theatre Conference (SETC),

which have auditions/interviews every year around the country. At the SETC conventions, theatres from all over the country hold interviews. It is a very affordable way to get your name and face seen by many professional companies.

Outdoor dramas have been around for years, are located from Texas to Ohio to North Carolina, and performing during the summer months. Most of them are epic pageants that deal with the American experience. They often offer classes for their cast/crew in theatre—including combat (e.g. my experience at *Tecumseh!*).

SM EXPERIENCE: As a stage manager, I worked in four states on five outdoor dramas. I believe it is one of the best teaching tools for young stage managers. You have to deal with a different problem every day of the week. You are constantly putting in understudies, and you even have to contend with Mother Nature. Plus, they are a lot of fun.

Some summer theatres are repertory companies, which produce four or five productions (usually musicals) in a two-month period. You spend your days rehearsing and your evenings in performance. It is hard work, but you learn a lot—quickly.

There are numerous summer Shakespeare Festivals. They are also looking for young stage managers to serve as ASMs, and possibly, to stage manage a "second season" of shows (e.g. intern performances).

THE JOB HUNT

When you start looking for a job as a stage manager BackstageJobs.com and Theatre Communications Group's ARTSEARCH are both useful sources. SETC also lists jobs throughout the year in their job contact service.

When you first enter the professional theatre, keep in mind that you are one of many seeking work. Don't assume that just because you were a big fish in your college pond, producers and directors will be knocking down your door to hire you.

Most stage managers start their careers working as an assistant stage manager. You may succeed in working at an Equity theatre for your first professional job, but more likely you will work for a non-Equity professional theatre.

Once you start working in the professional theatre, keep in contact with everyone—lighting designers, producers, directors, and even actors. Networking is the way to find your future jobs. Actors Equity has a site with job listings once you are a member of the union, but a lot of the best jobs never make it to the listing. It is so much "who you know". Keep a listing of email addresses and don't let people forget you.

RÉSUMÉ

Whether you are applying for an Equity assistantship or a community theatre stage management position, you must have a well thought out résumé. In the theatre we use a one-page format. The person hiring does not want to see a listing of every job you have ever done: pick and choose the most important ones.

When you are just graduating from college, your résumé will include the college stage management work (including student directed productions), and related theatre work while at the college (e.g. master electrician). Your technical experience is very important, and should show that you are well versed in all aspects. Appendix Two gives you an example of a résumé of someone who is graduating from college with some professional experience.

Never lie on your résumé. The theatre world is a small one (everybody knows everybody).

COVER LETTER

You should also have a simple cover letter to go with your résumé. Do your homework and address the letter to the person responsible for hiring stage managers. Keep the letter succinct. Make sure to point out your strengths as a stage manager. If you have done your homework, you can point out why you would be a positive member of the company. Don't try to make yourself out to be the world's best stage manager.

Don't expect to get replies from every theatre to which you apply. Don't narrow your field to one or two theatres and ignore the rest. Keep sending out your résumé and cover letters.

> SM TIP: Stage managers are hired early in a production. For summer work, you should be sending out your résumé and cover letter in January (at the latest).

INTERVIEWS

If you are lucky enough to be granted an interview, make sure to be yourself. Don't try to fool anyone. If they ask you a question about a situation in which you have never been involved, don't lie. Tell them that you have never had that experience, but tell them how you *would* deal with it. Always take extra copies of your résumé to your interview.

ACTORS' EQUITY ASSOCIATION

Actors' Equity Association (AEA/Equity) is the union of actors and stage managers. You do not want to join Equity until you are ready to take on the responsibility of stage managing in a pressure-filled environment. The benefits of being a member of Equity are many (not the least of which is health and pension benefits). *But*, once you are a member, you are not allowed to work non-union shows. This is an important decision, for which you need to be fully prepared.

There are two ways to get into the union as a stage manager: get hired to stage manage at an Equity theatre/show, or through the Equity Membership Candidate program.

EQUITY MEMBERSHIP CANDIDATE PROGRAM

Many professional Equity theatres participate in the Equity Membership Candidacy (EMC) Program. Through EMC, young stage managers work for one of the theatres for 50 weeks as an assistant stage manager. After the requirements are met, they are then eligible to join Equity. If you go to the AEA website, you will find a list of the theatres around the country that participate. In addition, you will find the requirements of the program. You have to pay to join the EMC program.

JOINING EQUITY

When you get hired to stage manage for an Equity company, you then *must* join Equity. It is as simple as that. The trick is getting the Equity company to want to hire you. They will not be looking to hire a stage manager right out of college. They will expect that you have worked in the professional theatre for several years.

SM EXPERIENCE: I "got my card" (Equity membership card) by getting a Theatre for Young Audiences tour. I had been stage managing professionally for ten years. During that time, I had worked as a stage manager in numerous regional theatres (and outdoor dramas), and on many Equity showcases in New York (where I was the *only* non-union member in the company). When I got my contract, the producer who hired me, said that I was "overqualified" for the position on a TYA tour. He may have been right, but I had been enjoying working non-union all around the country. (Remember, everyone's story is different.)

If you live in the New York, Chicago, or Los Angeles area, once you get hired, you take your contract to the Equity offices. They will then enroll you in the union, and arrange for the payment of membership dues. It is at this time, that you choose your "Equity name". If you live outside those areas, you will mail your contract to the office required on their website.

JACK-OF-ALL-TRADES

If you take the time to learn the other technical aspects of theatre, you have added to your ability to get a job as a stage manager. Some theatres want a stage manager that can also run the light board. They will have someone in the company that will hang and focus the lights, and program the board, but they need someone to run the light board during performances. Or maybe they will contract you to start a few weeks early to help build the set.

In special circumstances, you might have to take over running sound or lights during a show because someone is absent (e.g. due to illness). If you have the background and knowledge to work in many areas, you become much more desirable as a stage manager.

The Theatre for Young Audiences contract with Equity is a great way for young stage managers to get into Equity. But, you need to be able to work the technical aspects, because the shows depend on the stage manager to be the technical director on tour, and often, the sound board operator as well.

CHAPTER TWELVE

☑ SOME FINAL THOUGHTS

You have now discovered the key to success as a stage manager: hard work. It is my belief (biased as it is), that stage managers are the hardest workers in the theatre. I would like to leave you with some final thoughts.

COMPUTERS
As a stage manager, a computer is of the utmost importance (a laptop is preferred). You need to be able to work on computer systems such as Word and Excel, as all your forms and sheets will need to be done on a computer. In addition, you can use your laptop in rehearsals to run sound cues, or to time scenes and set changes. The more accomplished you are with a computer, the more you can do to your lists and forms. Color-coding sections can help differentiate aspects within all your forms. And of course, if you have the computer next to you in rehearsal, you can input information as the rehearsal is actually happening. Be careful, some directors don't want to hear the clapping of the keyboard during rehearsals. You should keep that work to break times.

STAGE MANAGERS ARE NOT DIRECTORS
You may have the ultimate goal of directing, but when you work as a stage manager, you are not the director. You do not give the actors notes during rehearsal. If you give them

notes during the run of the show, it is to keep the director's vision intact. You do not make changes to that vision.

You must always see yourself as the director's right-hand-person: you are the one organizing their vision; you need to understand it, help them to translate it to the stage, and support them through the process (even if you *disagree* with that vision.) It is your job to show the cast and crew that you support the director. Talking behind a director's back with any other member of the company will only serve to eat away at the cohesion of the company.

SELF-EVALUATION

Every time you do a show, you need to finish with a self-evaluation: What did I do right? What did I do wrong? What is my weakness? After your self-evaluation, you need to work on your weaknesses. If your handwriting is bad, you have to work on it, because others *have* to be able to read your writing. Always have an open mind and be willing to learn from those around you. Let that help you develop as a theatre artist.

YOUR FUTURE

I tell my students that I'm not perfect, and neither are they. Do not take the information in this book as gospel. You must remember that this is *my* idea of what the job of the stage manager entails. It is from *my* experience of over thirty years of teaching and working as a professional stage manager. I hope that you use this as a springboard to your own ideas about how to be an effective and successful stage manager. And remember: theatre is a living organism. It takes a lot of people working together to keep it alive.

There is no way to secure your future as a stage manager. All you can do is *work hard* and *keep learning*. Be ready to travel while you learn. There are a lot of theatres out there.

"Break a leg".

APPENDIX ONE

☑TOOLS OF THE TRADE

CONTENTS of Stage Management KIT

OFFICE SUPPLIES:
   Highlighters (two or three different colors)
   Pencils
   Pencil Sharpener
   Eraser (Artist's Eraser recommended)
   Ruler
   Post its (several colors/sizes/shapes)
   Scotch Tape
   Letter size Paper
   Stapler
   Scissors
   Permanent Marker
   Pens
   Glue Sticks
   Clipboard

SPECIALTY ITEMS:
   USB Drive
   Spike tape (two or three colors)
   Gaffers Tape
   Glow tape
   Sanitary Napkins (or tampons)
   Kleenex

Hot Glue Gun with glue sticks
Extension Cord
Measuring Tapes (at least 2 at 25')

TOOLS
Hammer
Screwdrivers (Phillips and Regular)
Small screwdriver for glasses
Adjustable c-wrench
Mat Knife

EQUIPMENT NEEDS
Stopwatch
Computer (laptop suggested)
Cell phone
CD Player, MP3 Player or IPOD
Battery Charger
Printer (color suggested)
Headset/Clear Com belt pack
Littlelite or musician's clip on light for music stand

FIRST AID KIT
If the theatre does not have a first aid kit, you should suggest that they purchase a small one from the local pharmacy. It will come equipped.

In your stage management kit, you should also keep the following:
Ice Packs
Band Aids
Antibiotic ointment

APPENDIX TWO

☑ Résumé example

YOUR NAME
Address/Phone number
STAGE MANAGER

PROFESSIONAL WORK: (paid theatre work)
Stage Manager	Show *Title* (Co.)	2009
Master Electrician	*Title* (Company)	2007-08
Technician	*Title* (Company)	2006

EDUCATIONAL WORK:(School/degree/dates)
Stage Manager	*La Traviata*	Guest Director
	The Serpent	Graduate Student
	The Miser	Faculty Director
Assistant Director	*Man of La Mancha*	
Director	*California Suite*	
Lighting Designer	*Mr. Scrooge*	
	An Evening of Dance V	
Master Electrician	*An Evening of Dance IV*	
Lighting/Set Crew	Numerous shows	

Related Coursework: (e.g. lighting)
Related Work: (that shows management skills)
Driver's License (manual transmission)
Computer: Excel, Word, Powerpoint

GLOSSARY

Apprenticeship: A position (sometimes paid) that gives a person an opportunity to work with and learn from professionals.

Architect's Ruler: A specialized ruler used by architects and engineers to read plans without needing to use complicated mathmatical equations.

Artist's Eraser: A vinyl eraser that is designed to be non-abrasive so that it will not remove paper as it removes pencil marks.

Assistant Stage Manager: The person whose job is to help the stage manager with running rehearsals and organizing the show. Often the person who runs the deck during technical rehearsals and performances.

Audition: The process of actors either performing scenes or monologues for a director & producer in the hopes of being cast in a show.

Audition Form: A sheet that actors need to fill out when auditioning for a show that includes contact information and conflicts.

Audition Notice: A flyer that is posted around a campus/town to advertise when and where auditions will be held.

Audition Pictures: In lieu of, or in addition to, headshots, pictures taken with a digital camera at the time of auditions of each actor.

Audition Scenes (aka Sides): Scenes from the play that the director has chosen to be distributed to the auditionees for them to "perform" at the audition.

Background Sound: Ambient sounds that run under a scene (e.g. crickets, rain, etc.).

Backstage: The area of the stage that the audience cannot see.

Bio: Biography that each member of the cast, crew and staff must write for the program.

Blackout: The stage lights go out suddenly (i.e. "in a zero count").

Blacks: Curtains used to mask (hide) areas from the view of the audience.

Blind Entrance: An actor cannot see the stage and their entrance is based on a visual cue and not a line.

Blocking: 1) The process of the director giving the actors the movement that they wants for the play. 2) The movement the actor does in the play.

Blocking Notation: The written shorthand notes of the blocking the director assigns.

Blues: The blue colored lights used backstage so that actors/crew can see to do their jobs.

Body Mics: Microphones that are individual for each performer that do not have to be held in a hand.

Book: The script of a musical.

Booth: The part of the theatre from which the stage manager calls the show; it houses the light board (and sometimes the sound board and/or projector controls).

Break: Taking time off from rehearsal, for five or ten minutes.

Budget: 1) The money that is going to be spent for the production. 2) The amount of money that is alloted to the stage manager for supplies in relation to the production.

Building: The process of constructing the set.

Call: The time that a cast &/or crew member needs to be at a rehearsal or a performance.

Callback: The process of seeing actors a second or third time, after the initial audition, in order to read them in scenes or with other actors.

Callboard: Usually a cork board mounted in the theatre or in the rehearsal space for posting of important information (e.g. rehearsal schedule).

Calling Cues: The process of the stage manager telling the light board operator, the sound board operator and any other persons running tech when they should take a cue.

Cast List: An alphabetical listing of the actors and the characters they are playing in the show.

Center Line: The imaginary line down the center of the set that divides it into two halves.

Changing Booth: A backstage area cordoned off with curtains (complete with mirror and hooks for clothes) for use in changing costumes out of the view of cast and crew.

Character Descriptions: The director's short description of each of the characters that is distributed at auditions.

Cheat Sheet: A sheet that the lighting designer gives the master electrician that shows all the lights and where on the stage they should be focused.

Choreographer: The person hired to determine all the dance moves in the production and instructs the performers in those moves.

Combatants: Those actors that are involved in any stage combat.

Company Handbook: A handout that describes the theatre company and any rules or regulations that are followed by the company.

Conflicts: Any engagement (e.g. work, class, wedding) that would prevent an actor or crew member from being present at a rehearsal or performance.

Contact Sheet: An alphabetical listing of each member of the company with their contact information (phone numbers and email addresses).

Costume Change: An actor must change their costume between scenes/acts or within a scene.

Costume Fitting: An actor must meet with the costume designer in order to try on their costumes to see if they need to be altered.

Costume Parade: All of the actors get into their costumes for each act and the director and costume designer look at them under the stage lights.

Cover Letter: A letter written to a potential employer that states your interest in a position and why they should hire you.

Crew: The people working on all the technical aspects of the production.

Cue: 1) The number/letter of the lights or sound that is changing at any given moment in the show. 2) The actual line of dialogue when an actor/crew person must do something.

Cue Lights: Colored lights that are hung backstage and controlled from the booth by the stage manager in order to cue movements of the set.

Cue Line (aka Cue): The line of dialogue which is the moment a light or other technical aspect needs to be accomplished.

Cue Script: The stage manager's script containing only the written cues for running the show.

Cue-to-cue: A technical rehearsal where you jump from one technical cue to the next, skipping large portions of dialogue if there are no cues during it.

Curtain Down: The time each performance ends.

Curtain Up: The time each performance starts.

Curtain Warmers: Lights that are specifically focused on the front curtain while the audience is entering the theatre.

Cyc: A white drop around the back of the stage where the lighting designer focuses lights for a sky.

Daily Schedule: A listing of all the scenes and actors needed at any time for rehearsal for a specific day.

Dance Captain: The member of the company (usually a dancer), whose job it is to keep the dances up to the level they were when the show opened.

Deck: The stage floor.

Designers: Those people who are responsible for determining how the technical aspects (i.e. set, costumes, sound, and lights) are going to be for a production.

Down Stage: 1) The part of the stage that is closest to the audience. 2) A direction that is toward the front edge of the stage.

Dress Rehearsal: A rehearsal where the actors will wear their costumes and all technical aspects are already incorporporated.

Dress Tech Rehearsal: A rehearsal where the actors will wear their costumes and all the technical aspects of the show will be worked in and assigned.

Drop: A cloth that is painted with a scene and either hung upstage or flown in and out from above.

Dry Tech Rehearsal: A technical rehearsal that does not include actors.

Electrical Plots: The papers where the lighting designer notes the lighting instruments that are to be hung and focused.

Equity: Actor's Equity Association - The Union of Actors and Stage Managers.

Escape Stairs: Steps that are placed backstage, leading to/from a platform for the actors to use.

Fade Down: To make the lights or sound grow fainter until it reaches a designated intensity in a specific amount of time.

Fade In: To make the lights or sound grow more intense from silent until it reaches a designated intensity in a specific amount of time.

Fade Out: To make the lights or sound grow fainter until it disappears in a specific amount of time.

Fade Up: To make the lights or sound grow more intense until it reaches a designated intensity in a specific amount of time.

Fight Captain: The member of the company (usually a cast member who does combat), whose job is to keep the fights up to the level they were when the show opened.

Fight Director: The person hired to determine all the fight moves in the production and instruct the actors on them.

Final Drawings: The finished drawings for the set design.

Final Dress Rehearsal (aka Final Dress): The last dress rehearsal before opening night.

Fitting: When an actor must meet with the costume designer in order to try on their costumes to see if they need to be altered.

Floor Plan: The paper that shows the set design within the theatre from a bird's eye perspective.

Fly Crew: Those members the running crew who's responsibility is to fly the set pieces.

Fly Rail: The ropes attached to the series of weights and counter-weights used to raise and lower drops and electrics.

Fly Space: The area above the stage where there are pipes that can be raised or lowered.

Flying: The process of raising or lowering set pieces from the fly space to the deck.

Spot Ops: Those members of the running crew who operate the follow spots.

French Scene: Breaking the play down into scenes based on the entrance or exit of a character.

Ghost Light: A light that is placed center stage after a performance and turned on, so that there is a light in the theatre at all times. Sometimes it is permanently placed in the fly space and/or above the audience seating.

Giving Calls: Going around from "half hour" until "places" telling the actors and crew how much time they have remaining until places is called.

Giving Lines: Telling an actor what the correct line is when they call for line during a rehearsal.

Glow Tape: Tape that is used around the set and backstage that glows so that during a blackout an actor doesn't run into a set piece.

God Mic: A microphone for use by the stage manager that is heard throughout the theatre including backstage and the dressing rooms.

Green Room: The room designated backstage for the actors and crew to hang out in before, during and after a performance.

Hang and Focus: The time designated for hanging the lights in the theatre and focusing them on the stage.

House: The theatre's auditorium where the audience sits.

Equestrian: A person who's responsibility is to take care of any horses used in a production.

Headsets: The communication system used to communicate from the booth to backstage and possibly the house or box office.

Headshot: A picture that an actor uses to publicize themself.

House Manager: The person who is in charge of the ushers and determines when the house opens to the audience.

House Lights: Those lights that are above/around the audience so they can see to enter.

House Open: The time the theatre is open for the audience to enter and sit.

House Out: When the house lights fade to black.

House to Half: When the house lights fade from full to half.

Housing: Living accomodations that may be given to cast and crew members while they are working for a theatre.

Industrial: A performance (possibly a tour) that is sponsored by and for the purposes of promoting a business.

Intermission: The break between the acts in a performance.

Internship: A position (sometimes paid) that gives a person an opportunity to work with and learn from professionals.

Key: A listing of shorthand symbols used in a script (e.g. L for lights).

Light Board: The computer that is used to control the lights.

Light Board Op: The crew member who is responsible for running the light board.

Light Check: The master electrician goes through all the lights to make sure none has burned out since the last performance.

Lights Up: When the lights on the stage go from out to up for a scene.

Line of Sight: Anything that can be seen by either the director or the audience.

Line Through: Rehearsal where actors go through the script saying their lines but without blocking, props, etc. (usually held in the green room or a similar room.)

Lines: The words that the actors say in a play.

Masking: Curtains or other material that is set up to hide the backstage area from the audience.

Master Electrician: The person responsible for hanging and focusing the light plot.

Mat Knife: A utility knife used to cut.

Measurements: When the costumer and their assistant measure the actors so they can build costumes that fit them.

Measuring Tape: A retractable tape for use in spiking the set.

Meet and Greet: 1) A time set aside during the first rehearsal to allow each member of the company to give their names and maybe say something about themselves. 2) A time set aside at the first rehearsal to allow the actors, director, designers and anyone else present to stand around and talk.

Monitors: Speakers set backstage and in the dressing rooms to allow the cast and crew to hear the show as it happens.

Monologue: A long passage in a play spoken by one actor; actors often use monologues as an audition piece.

Multiple Floor Plan Sheet: A sheet that has several floor plans on it so the stage manager can notate where actors are to be at any moment during the play.

Music Director: The person hired to coordinate the musicians and teach the performers the music in the show (may or may not be the conductor).

Musical Numbers List: A listing of all the musical numbers in a show.

Off Book: The memorization of the lines in the script.

Off Stage: The area of the stage not in the sight lines of the audience.

Orchestra Pit: The area (sometimes under the stage) where the orchestra will be playing during the performance.

Paging a Curtain: Holding a curtain back for an actor.

Paging an Actor: Using the God mic to call an actor to the stage.

Performance Notes: Notes that the stage manager takes during a performance.

Performance Report (a.k.a. Performance Log): A listing of the performance notes as well as the times of the performance and any understudies that performed.

Photo Shoot: The taking of pictures of scenes from the show with the actors usually in costume.

Places: The call for when the actors should be in their proper places backstage, ready to make their first entrance and for when the crew should be in their places ready to run the show.

Post Show Checklist: The stage manager's list of jobs to be completed following each performance.

Preliminary Design: The first drawings that a designer will do to show the director their ideas of the design.

Preliminary Set Change List: The first list the stage manager puts together showing all the set changes in chronological order.

Preproduction: Any work that is accomplished prior to the first rehearsal.

Preshow: Anything that happens after the house opens and before the curtain is up.

Preshow Announcement: The speech given to the audience prior to curtain up that informs them of any rules or regulations of which they need to be aware.

Preshow Checklist: The stage manager's list of jobs to be completed prior to each performance.

Previews: Performances before a live audience prior to the official opening of a production.

Principal: A lead actor in an Equity show.

Production Contact Sheet: An alphabetical listing of each member of the creative staff with their contact information (phone numbers and email addresses).

Production Manager: The person responsible for coordinating all the technical aspects of a production.

Production Meeting: A meeting with the creative staff of a production.

Production Schedule (aka Production Calendar): An overview schedule that covers all rehearsals and performances and lists all the technical deadlines for a production.

Prompt Script: The script used by the stage manager to write down the blocking and keep track of all the technical aspects of a production.

Prop List: A listing of all the props used in a production.

Prop Master/Mistress: The person responsible for finding and building the props needed for a show.

Prop Running List: A detailed listing of all the props used in a production: where they are placed, when they move and who is responsible for the movement.

Prop Table: A labeled table set up backstage that is exclusively for placing props so that actors can find them when needed.

Publicity Call: When members of the company are called for an interview to discuss the show or to perform a section of the show.

Pyrotechnics: Explosions or smoke used in the show.

Pyrotechnician: The person responsible for the setting and safety of all pyrotechnics used in a production.

Quick Change: A costume change within a very short period of time, that usually needs the help of a wardrobe person in order to be accomplished.

Reader: A person whose job it is to read scenes with an auditionee.

Rehearsal: The time period from the beginning until the end when the show is being worked on by the director and/or the designers and/or the actors.

Rehearsal Pieces: Costume pieces that are used during rehearsal as a stand in for the actual costume.

Rehearsal Prop: Something that is used during rehearsals as a stand in for the actual prop.

Rehearsal Report (aka Rehearsal Log): A log of everything that happened during a rehearsal in addition to any notes the director may have given for the creative staff.

Rehearsal Scene: Breaking up of the play into parts that have been designated as complete scenes for rehearsal purposes.

Rehearsal Schedule: A listing of all the scenes - and actors needed for those scenes – that are to be rehearsed at a particular date and time.

Rehearsal Set Pieces: Set pieces that are used during rehearsals as a stand in for the actual set pieces.

Rehearsal Space: The space where rehearsals are held before moving into the theatre.

Rendering: A drawing of the set or costume designs from the perspective of the audience.

Repertory: A theatre company that presents a number of works, in rotation, during a season.

Résumé: A one-page listing of a person's important information about their theatre work history in order to pursue employment.

Run Through: To perform the entire play, in rehearsal, without stopping for mistakes.

Running Crew: Those members who are responsible for the technical aspects of the show during performance.

Running List: A listing of all the technical aspects of a production, when each is performed, and who is responsible for the move.

Running Time: The time it takes to run the show from curtain up to curtain down (including intermission).

Scale: Relating a measurement on a floor plan (or other design plans) to the actual set. Usually, theatre drawings have a scale of 1 foot equal to ¼ inch, ½ inch or sometimes 1 inch.

Scenario: A sequence of possible events.

Scene Breakdown: A listing of every scene in the play and every character that is in that scene.

Scene Change Sheets (aka Scene Shift Sheets): A floor plan that has been reduced to fit on letter size paper, on which is notated the moves of the set during a scene change and possibly the person responsible.

Scene Work Log: A listing of all the scenes in the play and what work has been accomplished on each scene during the rehearsal process.

Set Changes: The movement of set pieces during transitions between scenes or during scenes themselves.

Set Pieces: Any piece of furniture that is used during the show.

Setting: Where the play takes place.

Sequence of Cues: A number of cues that are connected by actions or lines.

Shorthand: A method of writing blocking and cues using symbols to represent words.

Showcase: A performance of a new work with a limited budget for sets and the other technical aspects.

Sides: 1) Specific scenes that have been pulled out of a play for audition purposes. 2) The script of a musical that only has cue lines and a characters own lines in it.

Sign In Sheet: A listing of the cast and crew and dates for each rehearsal or performance with a space for them to initial when they have arrived.

Sitzprobe: The first rehearsal with the actors and the orchestra with everyone seated in order to sing through the entire score with the orchestra.

Sound Board: The computer that is used to run sound cues and control microphones.

Sound Board Op: The person responsible for operating the sound board.

Sound Check: The sound board operator goes through all the microphones and speakers to make sure all elements of the sound system are working.

Sound Levels: The setting of the sound cues as to how loud or soft they are to run.

Specials: Lights that have a special purpose in the production (e.g. a glow from a box or an area on the stage where an actor is in a pool of light).

Spike Tape: Colored tape that is used to mark where set pieces are to be on the stage.

Spiking the Set: The process of putting spike tape on the deck to mark all the pieces of furniture.

Standby: What the stage manager says to the running crew prior to giving a cue (e.g. lights or sound) to get them ready.

Stage Combat: Any slaps, pushes or fighting that is performed by actors in a show.

Stage Directions: Those movements that are included in a published script from the original production.

Stage Left: 1) The area of the stage to the left of the center line from the actor's viewpoint as they face the audience. 2) A direction toward the stage left wings.

Stage Right: 1) The area of the stage to the right of the center line from the actor's viewpoint as they face the audience. 2) A direction toward the stage right wings.

Stage Management Kit: A container that holds the special tools needed by a stage manager such as pencils, reading light, etc.

Stock: The costumes and set pieces that a company will keep in storage to use on future productions.

Stop and Go Rehearsal: A rehearsal where the action is stopped, worked and then repeated.

Strike: The process of taking apart and/or tearing down the technical aspects after a show has closed.

Table Work: The director works with the actors on the script while seated at tables (usually prior to blocking the show).

Tech Table: A table or two set up in the house for the creative staff and stage manager from which they run the technical rehearsals.

Technical Director (TD): The person responsible for accomplishing all the technical aspects of the production.

Technical Rehearsal: Any of a number of rehearsals where the focus is on adding technical aspects to a production.

Timings: The using of a stop watch to get accurate running times of scenes, acts and the whole play.

Timing Sheet: A listing of each scene and act with slots to put in the running time of each during run throughs or performances.

Toggle Switch: An electrical switch that allows the stage manager to turn something (usually a light) on or off in another part of the theatre in order to cue a set change or entrance.

Transition: The time needed to move from one set to the next during a performance.

Trap: An opening in the stage floor, to allow for entrances and exits under the stage.

Understudy: An actor that is charged with learning the lines and movement of another actor so that they can replace that actor in a case where they are sick or absent from a performance.

Unit Set: A play that only has one setting, or a design that uses one setting.

Up stage: 1) The part of the stage that is farthest from the audience. 2) A direction that is toward the back of the stage.

Visual Cue: A signal for a move that has to be seen in order to accomplish it.

Wardrobe Crew: The persons responsible for quick changes and the upkeep of all costumes.

Weekly Schedule: A listing of all the scenes and actors needed at any time for rehearsal for a specific week.

Wings: The area off-stage right and off-stage left behind the masking.

Work Station: Any area that one designates where either the technical staff or stage manager will be working.

Working a Scene: When the director wants to stop and start a specific scene giving notes to the actors throughout the process.

Writing Cues: The time taken to write in the stage manager's script and input into the light board and sound board the changes throughout the production.

INDEX